CLASSICAL ARCHITECTURE

CLASSICAL ARCHITECTURE
RULE AND INVENTION

Thomas Gordon Smith

↴P

GIBBS M. SMITH, INC.
A PEREGRINE SMITH BOOK

Copyright © 1988 by Gibbs M. Smith, Inc.

First edition printed 1988

92 91 90 89 88   5 4 3 2 1

This is a Peregrine Smith Book, published by
Gibbs M. Smith, Inc., P.O. Box 667, Layton, UT
84041

Design by J. Scott Knudsen
Printed and bound in Hong Kong by Everbest Printing Co., Ltd.
through Asiaprint Limited, Laguna Niguel.
**Library of Congress Cataloging-in-
Publication Data**
Smith, Thomas Gordon, 1948—
     Classical architecture.

     Bibliography: p.
     1. Smith, Thomas Gordon, 1948— —Sources.
2. Classicism in architecture. 3. Smith,
Thomas Gordon, 1948— —Philosophy. I. Title.
NA737.S578A35 1988   720'.92'4   86-17668
ISBN 0-87905-246-5

TO MARIKA

TABLE OF CONTENTS

PREFACE

Few contemporary architects have engaged in such a direct revival of the classical language of architecture as Thomas Gordon Smith. To the eyes of his detractors, his designs appear bizarre and dangerously near kitsch. To his supporters, Smith's brightly decked "monumental houses" are a sharp slap in the bloodless face of late-modernism. His work takes great pleasure in representational ornamentation. While it has a more immediate appeal than that of the strict historicists, it is more rigorous in the literal detail of classical architecture than that of the postmodernists. Unlike Quinlan Terry, for example, who follows the eighteenth-century model academically, Smith moves the elements out of a historical context by combining them with the forms and materials of the contemporary vernacular. On the other hand, his risky experiments are different from his American counterparts. Michael Graves, for instance, does not employ literal quotation in his buildings, but makes referential paraphrases in which abstract ornament brings historical vocabulary "up to date." Smith argues that this vocabulary is not "historical" and insists that the forms of classical architecture can be a vital medium for architectural expression today *if* they are employed in a literate manner.

My first exposure to Thomas Gordon Smith was in 1978. A group of architectural historians was talking about contemporary architecture. One of the group told us about a young architect in California who was making "new baroque" buildings. How could this be happening today? I next heard of Smith from members of a symposium on Aalto's buildings in Finland during the summer of 1980. His name was controversial due to his inclusion on the *Strada Novissima* at the Venice Biennale. I resolved to go to Venice to see the baroque work of this enfant terrible.

Walking into Thomas Gordon Smith's exhibition, I confronted the model of a baroque oratory. The walls around it were hung with large watercolors of what seemed to be a seventeenth-century Roman church. The project turned out not to be a reconstruction of a historical building, but a proposal for a new church on a site in Rome. Smith had been impressed by baroque architecture for years and had made the surprising decision to adopt it as the point of reference for his own construction. The oratory project was as dangerously close to becoming baroque as Quinlan Terry's houses were to becoming eighteenth-century English estates. The asymmetrical plan of Smith's oratory, however, depends on the intervening insights of modern design seen in the curving "functionalist" plans of Hugo Häring.

Looking at the other projects presented in his exhibition at the Biennale, I could see that the originality with which Smith had translated his Italian studies in the oratory was also apparent in his earlier projects like the Doric and Paulownia houses. In the Paulownia project a classical arch was combined with a prefabricated quonset hut. Again and again, precious and exclusive symbols were placed against forms that were commonplace and secular.

This aspect of Smith's work owes a great debt to Robert Venturi and Charles Moore. Neither of these architects is willing to embrace classical architecture with whole-hearted acceptance of its literal forms or a commitment to permanence, but their liberating theories of the 1960s have been essential for perceiving it as an avenue for development. One can also agree with Charles Jencks that Smith's combination of opposites has its roots in the individualistic architecture of early twentieth-century Californians like Bernard Maybeck and Ernest Coxhead.[1] The regional roots of Smith's work, however, should not limit the applications of his message. He is now in Chicago and it will be interesting to see how his work will develop in the environment of Frank Lloyd Wright and Mies van der Rohe.

Smith's provocative design for Richmond Hill House responds to its northern California location, but it could certainly exist in other places around the globe. The baroque motifs of the facade are rendered with local techniques of construction that demonstrate Smith's realistic attitude; his practice of the classical tradition assumes utilization of the technology of our time. The introduction of baroque spatial movement in the cubic volume of the living room creates a plan that is at once referential and innovative. In this room (fig. 4.13f), the double oval of Dientzenhofer's eighteenth-century church is arranged on the diagonal to direct the vista toward distant Mt. Tamalpais. This irregular orientation contradicts the baroque principle of symmetry and, like the oratory, the room is conceivable only after the innovations of the 1910s and '20s.

Smith heightened the effect of this unusual volume by covering the curved black walls with frescoes derived from the Roman Third Style of painting. This is an example of his goal to reintegrate architecture with the richness of rhetorical painting. Smith consults with an art historian–iconographer, John Beldon Scott, to convey a subject through the painting. The frescoes at Richmond Hill represent the passage of time. The myth of Persephone, which explained the seasons for the Greeks, alludes to the cycle of the year, and the nine ages of man and woman are depicted on the ceiling to indicate the course of a lifetime. These images are meant to delight as well as to instruct.

Another component of this theme refers to millions of years. Richmond is an oil refinery center and tank farms and towers are visible from the living room along with the bucolic Mt. Tamalpais. Richmond's fossil fuel enterprise is indicated in the paintings in two ways. Petrolia, the goddess of the twentieth century's "black gold," is represented on the ceiling, and eight gasoline stations are painted on panels around the walls in the manner of Pompeiian pastoral vignettes. These little buildings chronicle our century by depicting the evolution of the gas station during its first eight decades.

The presence of an iconographic program, to say nothing of the symbolism of a room replete with an organ loft, suggests that Thomas Gordon Smith's intentions are not an ironic parody of the formality of classical architecture. In fact, the spiritual implications of this room underlie his belief that we must aspire to the classical principle of order to achieve a unified environment.

In this text on architectural theory Smith gives an account of his own work and upholds the long tradition of the architectural treatises. Wright, Le Corbusier, Gropius, and other outstanding architects of the twentieth century have also expressed their theories on architecture, but none would ever have taken up the Renaissance tradition of the *Säulenbücher,* or "Column Book." The principle of decorum, propounded as the central category of architectural theory by Vitruvius, was of no interest to them. They would have thought that nothing more could be made of the orders of columns. The early modernists were expressly opposed to this tradition, often engaging in polemic against it. What, then, made Thomas Gordon Smith take up the column after modernism had declared it obsolete?

Now that we have left the faceless constructions of outmoded modernism behind, we no longer see a building as a mere "container of functions." Architecture regains its capacity as art rather than engineering and has the freedom to become a poetic fiction. Robert Venturi said that "a building is a shed with ornament on it," reasserting the representational function of the facade, raising the question of what should be represented and how content should be expressed. Consequently, forms from the past were revived and used in conjunction with the current symbolic language, thus drawing a new intensity of meaning from the vocabulary of historical architecture and integrating it with the present. This set a curious game in motion: playing historical forms against modernist ones, thinking up surprising juxtapositions, and creating relationships between apparently irreconcilable elements. In its first decade from 1970, postmodern architecture was determined by these interesting attempts to create an ironic tension between the old and new by means of contrasts that loaded the building with meaning. Smith was an enthusiastic participant in this phase of postmodernism, and the Tuscan and Laurentian houses in Livermore display this friction between past and present, between grandiosity and simplicity. An example of this contradiction is the Greek akroterion that decorates the roof of Tuscan House. Despite its refined connotations, it is placed next to a common trough gutter.

Recently, Smith has made less and less use of this play of contrasts. He has recognized that it is dangerous in the long term to rely solely on wit, irony, and contradiction since they become arbitrary all too soon. When association becomes completely free, architectonic representation tends to become haphazard, and a combination only has to be as incredible as possible to emerge victorious. A building must be more than *just* interesting and its elements should not be free of syntax. Something of interest may attract attention, but it is not necessarily truthful. The German architect Gerd Neumann has designed a capital which is blown by the wind. It is an interesting image that derives its alienated form from the static Corinthian acanthus leaf. Smith rejects it, however, as a whimsical one-line joke incapable of repeated use.

Smith adopts the classical pair of opposites, *regula* and *invenzione,* to create a scale against which any degree of divergence may be measured. He is at pains not to become bound to the classical vocabulary of orders since that would make him rigid. Smith's application of historical forms initially arouses a feeling of recognition in the observer, who only then notices that there is something strange which does not correspond to his expectations. Confusion is produced and interrupts the process of identification. The traditional historical order is placed in relation to the *invenzione,* and its connotations cease to be unequivocal. In Smith's work the difference between the familiar and the unusual is very slight but of decisive importance. He succeeds in avoiding mere nostalgic revivalism, yet retains the *regula* to the greatest degree possible to prevent the invention from becoming arbitrary. Smith has chosen to walk a precarious and fascinating path.

Heinrich Klotz

ACKNOWLEDGMENTS

Many people have contributed to the development of this book directly and through long-term guidance. The research began during a year at the American Academy in Rome, and I am grateful to John D'Arms and the Directors of the Academy for creating an environment conducive to pursuing problems in design and research.

I owe special thanks to Heinrich Klotz as the book's patron. He gave it an incipient purpose in 1980 and his periodic evaluations have been of critical importance. In 1984 a grant from the Graham Foundation for Advanced Studies in the Fine Arts provided well-timed support for further research.

Many other architectural historians have provided inspiration and tolerant training. David Gebhard alerted me to the difference between plagiarism and emulation in architecture. The late John Ezra Beach warned of the foibles of "taste" and prepared the groundwork for a recognition of invention by teaching me to enjoy the vernacular of our century. Charles Jencks sharpened my arguments through discussions of the potential of classical architecture today. Vincent Scully's tacit belief in the role of the individual in architectural change has provided buoyant relief in the current atmosphere of "community." Christian Norberg Schulz has understood how and why the architecture of the seventeenth and eighteenth centuries might be a vital resource for design, and his steadfast insistence on the function of meaning and syntax in the classical system continues to challenge me. James Ackerman's admonitions have reinforced a determination which began by reading his *Palladio* many years ago.

In a similar sense, numerous architects have sponsored this book. Paolo Portoghesi has been a model for emulation. Philip Johnson has made insightful comments during periodic interchanges. Robert A. M. Stern has balanced criticism with support. Charles Moore has provided much help, and Robert Venturi's *Complexity and Contradiction* has been a resource and a paradigm for this publication. Finally, Stanley Tigerman has created a polemical atmosphere at the University of Illinois at Chicago that supports instruction in classical architecture.

Alex Gorlin, Andrew Hoyem, Elizabeth Snowden, Paul Fischberg, Blair and Helaine Prentice, James and Barbara Gordley and Barry Bergdoll have provided valuable comments on the manuscript. Gibbs M. Smith, Madge Baird, and Buckley Jeppson have provided invaluable editorial help. John Tittmann and Eric Doud have generously supplied drawings and Terrance O'Neil helped in organizing the illustrations. Hans Baldauf completed research for the reconstructions, and Georg Rattay translated Erik Forssman's *Dorisch, Jonisch, Korinthich* in order to make the ideas of this historian accessible to me.

My experience of rebuilding the San Francisco Architectural Club has paralleled my writing. I thank Michael Corbett, Frank Gerner, James Robertson, Carolyn Walker, Terrance O'Neil, Thayer Hopkins, Eliott Treister, Waverly Lowell, Mary Hardy, Charles Barrett, Assen Assenov, and Morgan Connoly for helping to make the S.F.A.C. classes an ideal forum for the ideas generated by this research.

I thank the librarians of the institutions in which this book was researched and written, especially the College of Environmental Design, the Art-History/Classics, and the Oriental Languages libraries at the University of California at Berkeley. The libraries of the American Academy, the Herziana in Rome, the Centro Palladio in Vicenza, and the Avery at Columbia University have been equally hospitable during my visits.

I have learned the importance of balancing rule and invention in the analogous world of music by studying with harpsichordist Jean Nandi and by following the revitalized baroque operas produced by Alan Curtis and Shirley Wynne.

Three colleagues who pursue similar goals in their own fields have provided much encouragement. Joseph Connors's interest in a wide range of topics that pertain to the culture of the baroque has alerted me to new avenues of exploration. The classicist Margaret Miles has been generous with ideas that are basic to the reconstructions of archaeological material. As an iconographic consultant, John Scott has suggested methods for developing my long-term intention to incorporate programmatic imagery in buildings. His kindness in measuring the blocks of the Hercules shrine in Rome demonstrates his commitment to this "worthiest of causes."

This book results from the early encouragement of my interest in architecture and travel provided by my parents, Sheldon and Margaret Smith. The opportunities to build afforded by my parents-in-law, James and Demetra Wilson, and my other clients have made those aspirations more concrete.

My children have shown remarkable tolerance for my work. The primary support has come from my wife, Marika, to whom this book is dedicated. Her patient editing and suggestions have made these pages more readable; her love of building inspires these arguments and motivates their realization.

INTRODUCTION

Modern conditions are treated as fixed, though the very word "modern" implies that they are fugitive. "Old ideas" are treated as impossible, though their very antiquity often proves their permanence.

G. K. CHESTERTON[1]

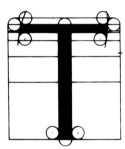

THIS BOOK ARGUES FOR THE REVIVAL OF CLASSICAL architecture as a medium for vital practice today. We must approach it with the radical intent of returning to its roots in order to synthesize a method for the form and theory of new classical buildings. We must turn our backs on the modernist mentality of alienation with a goal of restoring a sense of spirit to architecture (fig. I.1).

I propose that the classical tradition be revived as a force in the architecture of the twenty-first century. To achieve this, we must reject the primary modernist assumption that reduces everything to abstraction. Modernism alienates humans from God, art from technology, and separates our time from the past. Its limiting vision singles out "appropriate" responses to our culture and condemns all others. We are told not to imitate classical architecture because it is the product of a "different" historical context. This mentality denies the prospect of making spiritual bonds between ourselves and historical architects, a process that has always been essential for the vitality of architecture. More broadly, it inhibits the continuity of tradition. The modernist assumption is arrogant; it asserts that our period is so unique that we should not imitate our forebears in any tangible way.

The classical architect embraces continuity, both for the richness it gives the community and for the challenging standards it sets. Throughout its development, beginning 2,600 years ago, classicists have sought to emulate the achievements of an earlier age. Even the first buildings that demonstrate a recognizable classical system emulate the monuments of Egypt and the ancient Near East.[2]

To become a classical architect requires a commitment to scholarship. One must learn its formal systems of proportion and strive to understand its less tangible aspect:

I.1. Thomas Gordon Smith, Mathews Street House, Berkeley, 1978. View at dawn. (Collection of the Cooper Hewitt Museum).

the meaning of its forms and their potential for communication. Literacy is gained slowly by imitating models—the Greeks called them paradigms—and by testing them in the new applications encountered in architectural practice.[3] This initiates a lifelong study of buildings and theoretical writings motivated by a desire to delve more and more deeply into the variety of form while simultaneously attempting to consolidate consistent standards for practice.

Every classical architect whom I admire has not only practiced these artistic and scholarly dimensions but has developed spiritual qualities in buildings. Spirit is by nature amorphous, especially hard to grasp when associated with an abstract art like architecture. It is easiest to conceive as a component of sacred buildings which must convey a people's belief to be authentic. Synagogues, temples, mosques and churches should not merely function for the service; they must inspire a sense of the life-giving qualities that religion conveys through revealing the relationship between God and humankind. To achieve this, classical architects have at their disposal a vast tradition of architectural and figural elements that begin with the earliest monumental Greek temples. A sense of spirit should not be restricted to places of worship, however. Civic and residential buildings have an equal if less explicit potential to convey this quality. The anthropomorphic aspect of the column and the tradition of assigning a character to each order has long reinforced the spiritual and totemic aspect of classical architecture. This animating aspect of the word *spirit* must be infused into buildings. For the dwelling, Charles Moore termed this quality the "place" of houses.[4] Whatever spirit is called, it is an essential quality. With it, one

classical building is humane and approachable; without spirit, another is cold and forbidding.

While an architect must have a sensitive character to convey spirit and pursue scholarship, a resilient temperament is also necessary. No one is born with the divine wisdom of Athena. The aspiring classical architect must make an assumption of self-worthiness in spite of initial ignorance of the forms and methods of the classical system. This audaciousness must be maintained throughout practice, because one must contribute to this august tradition. Contributing entails pitting oneself against the standards of the great architects in history.

To revive classical architecture we must answer the allegation of the modernist that its systems, forms, and detail are neither valid nor possible any longer. We must not be timid in our response: the only effective way to counter the charge is to erect classical structures, the proof that classicism is of our time. The permanence and workmanship are available when we apply our knowledge and have the will of clients with vision.

While we can expect continued resistance from the legions of neo-modernists, we can also anticipate an increasingly supportive environment. There has been growing interest in classicism since the mid-1970s. The necessary adolescence of postmodernism is passing, and several interpretations of a new classicism have begun to mature. This is reinforced by parallel movements in other media such as music and painting. Equally important, bridges are being rebuilt with the field of archaeology, a legacy generally spurned by architects since the 1920s. As architects catch up with archaeological discoveries that provide new analysis of the origin and development of classical forms, both fields will be enriched. We can be grateful to modernism for one thing: it swept away the calcified practice of the late beaux- arts. This enables us to approach classical architecture in response to its larger history, rather than being dominated by a single facet of its development.

By constructing new classical buildings we will shift the critique from questions of appropriateness to the deeper one of authenticity. The key to achieving this quality is an understanding of the interrelation of rule and invention in history and practice.

MY INTRODUCTION TO CLASSICAL ARCHITECTURE

In my early teens I admired Frank Lloyd Wright's later buildings in San Francisco (fig. I.2), but I also attended monthly socials at a remarkable house in Berkeley—the Temple of Wings. This was the first classical structure that I experienced intimately. Over the years, I learned to see the building in many ways. On one hand, I sensed a special way of life it inspired and absorbed its lore. On the other, I saw it with increasing objectivity as architecture.

I.2. Frank Lloyd Wright, V. C. Morris Shop, San Francisco, 1949.

I.3. A. Randolph Monro and Florence Treadwell Boynton, The Temple of Wings, Berkeley, 1914. Florence Boynton and her children, c. 1915. (Courtesy OEloèl Quitzow Braun).

I.4. Arthur Matthews, *Youth*, c. 1917, 59½" x 67¾" with frame. (Collection of the Oakland Museum, gift of the Concours d'Antiques, Art Guild, the Oakland Museum Association.)

The Temple of Wings was built by Florence Treadwell Boynton between 1911 and 1914 (fig. I.3).[5] The house was an expression of the Craftsman mania for healthful, outdoor living and a testament to her friend, Isadora Duncan. Boynton shared Duncan's romantic vision of Greek culture, and the temple was a reflection of the San Francisco Bay Area's cultural identification with the classical Mediterranean. At this time the University of California was dubbed the "Athens of the West,"[6] and the paintings of Arthur Matthews combined the classical ideal with a California setting (fig. I.4).[7]

The Temple of Wings was composed originally of thirty-four concrete Corinthian columns modeled on the Choragic Monument of Lysikrates in Athens. The columns stood on a concrete stylobate warmed by radiant heat and supported a skylit roof. An enclosure stood within this hypostyle structure for a bathroom and for storage of books and pantry items. The kitchen was in open air. During inclement weather, canvas tarps protected the chiton-clad children from wind-driven rain.

Boynton's Temple of Wings met the ideal for an elemental classical building proposed by Laugier, an eighteenth-century French architectural theorist:

> *He wants to make himself a dwelling that protects but does not bury him. . . . The cold and heat will make him feel uncomfortable in this house which is open to all sides but soon he will fill in the space and feel secure.*[8]

In 1923 a fire swept through the Berkeley hills and destroyed the roof of the structure (fig. I.5). To rebuild the house, Boynton erected walls within the surviving peristyle and created two wings around a concave portico (fig. I.6).

When I first saw the Temple of Wings it

I.5. A. Randolph Monro and Florence Treadwell Boynton, The Temple of Wings. The concrete columns stand amidst the ruins of the 1923 fire. (Courtesy OEloèl Quitzow Braun.)

profoundly affected my sense of what architecture could be. My impressions are a synthesis of images of the house in its original state, combined with memories of the polychromed walls as they stand today. I learned that classicism did not have to be stiff and formal. I caught the living spirit of the building and the experience introduced me to the possibilities of a cultured life within the confines of a family home. It became a model for combining the intangible aspects of humanity and spirit within the "ancient" forms of classical architecture. These lessons were reaffirmed on my walks through the neighborhood to see Bernard Maybeck's classical–vernacular houses such as the Oscar Maurer Studio of 1907 (fig. I.7).

What I learned from the Boynton house lay dormant for a time, but in recent years I have found that this experience was similar to that of other avowed classicists. In the late 1950s, the composer Conrad Cummings became intrigued with the

sound of the harpsichord and learned to play it during his teens. At that time the harpsichord was considered unequivocally "historical," but its repertory created for

I.6. Florence Treadwell Boynton, Edna Deakin, and Clarence Casebolt Dakin, The Temple of Wings, Berkeley. Portico after 1924 remodeling.

I.7. Bernard Maybeck, Oscar Maurer Photographic Studio and residence, Berkeley, 1907. Detail of entry window with Doric taenia and guttae below.

I.8. Conrad Cummings, Psyche and her parents at the Oracle of Apollo, scene from *Eros and Psyche,* a three-act opera produced at Oberlin Conservatory, 1983. (Courtesy Oberlin College.)

Cummings an alternative to the preconceptions of modern musical tuning and form. On a trip to Greece in 1963, the painter David Ligare was struck by the light and sense of place that had nurtured classical culture. His impressions of the atmosphere, landscape and the subject matter of antiquity deeply influenced his later approach to painting.

CLASSICISM IN CONTEMPORARY MUSIC AND PAINTING

The intent, method, and effect of Cummings's and Ligare's work parallels my own, and their interpretations of classicism affirm the breadth of this movement. Conrad Cummings's opera *Eros and Psyche* of 1983 is a neo-baroque/neoclassical work that employs motifs from Monteverdi, Handel, and Mozart (fig. I.8).[9] He does not treat these sources as detached fragments as do his postmodern contemporaries, nor is he overly dependent on them. The historical material is woven together by a tonal system derived from the theory of Philip Glass; yet Cummings develops the character of his mythological subjects with comprehensible recitatives in emulation of baroque opera. At the same time he employs his experience in composing for electronic instruments by developing a synthesized voice for the Oracle of Apollo. The machine creates a voice that begins an octave above soprano and descends to an octave below bass, producing an androgynous vocal range for the god of music that would have delighted Handel. This high-tech singing is not used in an Orwellian sense to remind us that "Yes, we are in the twentieth century"; it is integrated with the opera to reinforce the emotional impact of the Pythian priestess and her message.

The paintings of David Ligare show a similar sensibility. Ligare renders the classical subjects of his sweeping pastorales with an intent to transmit extra-pictorial values.[10] The warmth that emanates from his paintings assures that they are neither a product of inanimate hyper-realism nor of the self-cancelling postmodern mentality. Ligare's *Allegorical Landscape (Nature and the Ideal)* preserves the subject matter of its working title, *Philosopher Teaching Social Responsibility* (fig. I.9). The seminar in the foreground is focused on the Pythagorean triangle inscribed in the soil. The evocative reconstruction of Pliny's Laurentian Villa by Leon Krier is depicted in the background as a small city. Ligare employed this well-known image of contemporary classical architecture to provide an inspired context for his primary lesson. Like Krier, he

believes that citizens should be responsible to each other and be guardians of their environment.

THE GOALS OF A TREATISE

This book presents a theoretical approach to employing the orders, it provides models drawn from historical examples, and it defines a canon of proportions for the orders. Finally, the presentation of my own designs demonstrates one approach to practicing classical architecture today.

These basics of theory, canon and paradigm must be presented again for practical and theoretical reasons. From the time of my earliest projects, I have relied on the books of Vitruvius, Palladio, and William Chambers to supply direction on how to proportion the orders.[11] Although

I.9. David Ligare, *Allegorical Landscape (Nature and the Ideal)*, 1986. Oil on linen, 78″ x 110″. (Courtesy David Ligare.)

authoritative, their approaches need to be revised today. Their units of measurement are no longer current, and the models they select for detail are confined to the archaeological knowledge of their time. For these reasons alone, a new canon must be established. In addition, none of the historical treatises can answer contemporary debate. The question of the appropriateness of classical elements for architecture today provides an atmosphere that has similarities to the past but also calls for new responses.

The historical illustrations I have chosen demonstrate the variety in the classical system. I admired these buildings long before I could commit myself to practicing architecture in a similar spirit, and I began to develop a theory through the attraction to particular buildings before I was aware of principles they share. At the same time, their diversity indicates the wide parameters that should be drawn for the term *classical*. What Pollitt has written for Greek sculpture defines my usage:

> *Classicism is "... an essentially conventional term ... devoid of any a priori value judgements ... let the term define itself by demonstration. By analysis of ... what unifies it in spite of its own considerable inner diversity, we can perhaps arrive at an appreciation of the word's significance. ..."*[12]

This book is not exhaustive. The reader should look elsewhere for a history of classical architecture. Summerson's *The Classical Language of Architecture*[13] is a wonderful introduction, and Onians's book on the classical orders will emphasize more advanced problems of interpretation and meaning in historical development.[14] Although the activity of other contemporary classical architects parallels my own,

their work is not included here.

The goal to develop a sense of spirit in architecture led me to the classical tradition. I would never have isolated a theory, defined the proportions of a canonical order, or looked to historical examples to help solve architectural problems if I had not been motivated by the questions arising from the challenge of practice.

When I began to design classical buildings, I struggled with the question of whether scholarship or design should dominate my time. I could not separate these interests as I began to realize that the architects who were my spiritual mentors had not separated history from their architectural production. On the contrary, they allowed their models to structure and inspire their work in an uninhibited way. Classical architecture demands integration of these factors and must be generated not only through drawing and study but through belief. Perhaps this is the unintentional gift of modernism: it forces those who believe that classical architecture is vital to make a statement of faith.

In this book I have tried to avoid the dogmatism underriding the concept of an architectural treatise, yet follow models of the authors cited earlier. None of them employed the word *classical* in the title or text of their works. They all took the Greek and Roman roots of their art for granted. Even such divergent architects as Guarino Guarini and William Chambers assumed "classical" when they titled their treatises *Civil Architecture*.[15] Today there are those who are breathing life into the ancient forms of this tradition again. Those who succeed are already thinking "classical" when they say "architecture."

**I.10. Carlo Maderno, Santa
Susanna, Rome, 1603.
(Sketch for measurements
by Thomas Gordon Smith.)**

TOWARD AUTHENTIC CLASSICAL ARCHITECTURE

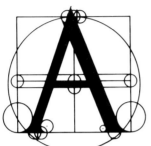

THE FUTURE OF THE CORINTHIAN ORDER pair of Corinthian capitals demonstrates two directions that the revival of classical architecture might take. The first is drawn in reaction to the worldwide movement of postmodernism. In 1980 the German architect Gerd Neumann made an exquisite drawing of a windblown Corinthian capital (fig. 1.2). His evocative idea was to represent a decomposed version of the canonical capital. At first glance, the drawing seems similar to the fanciful rococo capitals of Bavarian churches (fig. 3.31) or to stylized early Christian capitals like those at St. Simeon Stylities in Syria (fig. 3.54). Neumann's intentions, however, are different. The drawing conveys a negative message because he has subjected the decoration to hurricane-force gales that fatigue the bronze leaves beyond the point of springing back to their normal position.

For Neumann, the Corinthian capital is destitute of meaning. He maintains that "in the postmodern euphoria . . . the historical form of the column returns as an empty form . . ., not to the re-establishment of fully developed historical forms in the present."[2] This expression of the modernist mentality refuses to admit a classical element to the formal vocabulary of our time. As we will see in chapter 3, his attempt at constraint is futile; the Corinthian order has an unstoppable tendency to regenerate.

The alternative approach incorporates classical elements with a belief that they are valid. We cannot do this through reverential plagiarism, but we must unlock the Corinthian capital from its association as a "historical" form. This means following a difficult course between respecting the rule and authority of the canonical model and responding to the functions, themes, and technology of our own time.

1.1. Thomas Gordon Smith, Garden Court, Deutsches Architekturmuseum, Frankfurt, 1984. (Collection of the Deutsches Architekturmuseum.)

1.2. Gerd Neumann, windblown Corinthian capital, 1980. Pencil drawing. (Courtesy Heinrich Klotz.)

1.3. Thomas Gordon Smith, Corinthian capital, Garden Court, Deutsches Architekturmuseum, Frankfurt, 1984. Redwood and bronze.

The Corinthian capital in a small courtyard I designed at the Deutsches Architekturmuseum in Frankfurt aims to accomplish this goal (fig. 1.1). It is one of eleven cubicles allocated by the building's architect, Matthias Ungers, for permanent exhibits by a variety of architects.[3] Heinrich Klotz, the museum's director, assigned the courts asking for interpretations of "Adam's House," the archetypal shelter. The subject did not sit well with the modernists, who demanded freedom to do as they pleased. Once the requirement was dropped, I took the opportunity to refine the original theme and transformed the court into a shrine to Apollo, god of the sun and the arts. The dedication commemorates the spot where Daphne, fleeing the god's darker side, was transformed from a nymph into a laurel, Apollo's sacred tree. I was attracted to the theme because of the poignant implications of Daphne's transformation; it is comparable to the changes in artistic sensibility and values today, as well as an expression of the infusion of life into inanimate objects such as trees, columns or buildings.

The simple structure of the sanctuary is oriented toward the sun. An apselike hedge of myrtle surrounds a tree representing Daphne, a cross of the Greek *Laurus nobilis* and the bay laurel indigenous to California. In this hybrid plant, the cultural tradition of the Mediterranean is fused with the genes of the wild, but climatically similar, West. The dedication attempts to bring this universal story of unrequited passion to our time through the combination of plants and architectural symbols. The irony of making classicism manifest in Europe, even on this tiny scale, confronts a phenomenon of our time: like Neumann, most Europeans refuse to accept the Corinthian order as authentic; yet here it stands.

The Corinthian capital is the most elaborate element in this structure. Its bronze ornament is applied to a wooden bell and abacus (fig. 1.3). Its form derives from primitive capitals emphasizing the difference between the structural element and the superficial leaves which adorn it (fig. 3.33). The standard components are changed, however, to reflect the theme of the court. The leaves are the obligatory acanthus in the first register. In the second row the spearlike laurel leaves represent both Apollo and Daphne. The volute tendrils of the canonical Corinthian are replaced by a symbol of Apollo's sun—four flames that lick at the sharply pointed horns of the abacus.

This is the only classical structure at the museum. It is surrounded by ten courts that make equally personal statements. This capital does not fully satisfy my goal to resolve our culture with the standards of tradition, but it is a step in that direction. It achieves a positive result by respecting the integrity of the column and contributing to the regeneration of the Corinthian order.

A BAROQUE PARADIGM

The Composite capital, designed by Francesco Borromini in 1667 at the church of San Carlo alle Quattro Fontane, provides a historical model that sets a standard for preserving integrity while radically reinterpreting the canonical form (figs. 1.4, 1.5). At first this flamboyant capital looks similar to Neumann's; yet it respects the spirit of the canonical model in a way that his does not. The Borromini capital conveys a sense of calm, not chaos, and its variations are made to support the meaning of this church built for the Trinitarian order. The Trinitarian emblem—the Greek cross— replaces the fleuron typically located at the center of the abacus. The cross is framed

1.4. Francesco Borromini, Composite capital of the first register of columns, San Carlo alle Quattro Fontane, Rome, executed after 1667.

1.5. Francesco Borromini, facade, San Carlo alle Quattro Fontane.

by a laurel wreath, a symbol of victory. Borromini stripped the bell of vegetation and placed the crown of the Trinitarian co-founder, Saint Felix Valois, at the center. This attribute is intertwined with featherlike palm fronds that drape from unrolled volutes originating at the four corners of the abacus. The oak leaves that curl around the astragal may refer to Alexander VII, pope during the construction of the facade.[4] Borromini substitutes Christian symbols for the elements used in antiquity to give vitality to the ancient language of classical architecture. He enriches that language with the understanding of his contemporary culture by incorporating its symbols. We do not possess an iconology that explains the meaning of each element; yet we can still piece its message together. Not everyone may feel comfortable following Borromini's free and symbolic method, but his model challenges us to combine the elements of classical architecture with our own symbols.

To achieve Borromini's level of understanding, the classical architect must be multifaceted and combine technical and artistic capabilities with study of archaeology, theory, and iconography. The following case studies demonstrate models for how an architect can employ these interests to develop new structures. They also show how functional, artistic, and rhetorical concerns can be met in classical buildings. Finally, the vital interrelation between the architect and a visionary client is presented.

THE TEMPLE OF APOLLO AT THERMON: THE RESOURCES OF ARCHAEOLOGY

When I began to study architecture, I described my goal of integrating architectural history with architectural design to my advisor. He commented, "So you want to

be an applied archaeologist?" I began to realize that the classical architect's natural interest in history is contrary to one principle of modernism: the denial of the usefulness of the past. By contrast, classical architects want to create a bond with their predecessors. The historian or archaeologist might deplore the architect's inevitable lapses of objectivity, but the architect's intentions in studying history are different from theirs.[5] One goal is to learn the forms and methods of articulating classical vocabulary. Another is to develop a kindred tie with the mentality and spirit of model architects. The two basic sources for learning this tradition are buildings and books. Buildings can include the excavated foundations and fragments of archaeological remains, considered here, or structures that remain intact, as we will see in later sections. Both graphic material and written treatises supplement the buildings themselves.

One reason to study archaeology is to discover the origins of our "species." Although the process by which the orders evolved cannot be fully answered, architects, at least since the Hellenistic period, have been fascinated with questions of origin.

Curiosity about the development of the Doric order has usually been answered with the hypothesis that Doric forms represent wooden structural elements petrified into stone. Vitruvius argued for this interpretation:

In view of . . . carpenters' work generally, craftsmen imitated such arrangements in sculpture when they built temples of stone and marble. For they thought these models worth following up. Thus workmen of old . . . cut off the projections of the beams, as far as they came forward, to the line and perpendicular to the walls. But since this appearance was ungraceful, they fixed tablets shaped as triglyphs now are, against the cut-off beams, and painted them with blue wax, in order that the cut-off beams might be concealed so as not to offend the eyes. Thus in Doric structures, the divisions of the beams being hidden began to have the arrangement of the triglyphs, and between the beams, of metopes.[6]

Vitruvius's authority on this issue has had long-term influence on architects. The sixteenth-century Florentine Gherardo Spini painfully picked apart each element of the Doric entablature in his manuscript for a book on the structural origins of classical elements and attempted to illustrate the rationale of wooden guttae and triglyphs (fig. 1.6).[7] William Chambers's *Third Sort of Hut* is a theoretical archetype of the "original" temple based upon the same Vitruvian rationale (fig. 1.7).[8] Bringing Vitruvius's influence on this matter up to date, the contemporary architect Quinlan Terry executed a garden pavilion in the late 1970s based on the Chambers scheme. Some archaeologists have made desperate attempts to reinforce the Vitruvian theory by interpreting every canonical element of the Doric entablature in light of its supposed structural purpose (fig 1.8).[9] The problem with all of these efforts is they work backward from the artifact and force their theories of origin to comply with a legend.

Beginning at the turn of the century, discoveries at Thermon in northwestern Greece and the sites of other archaic temples revealed evidence which supports another interpretation of the origins of Doric architecture; that invention and cultural borrowing were the crucial factors in its development.

The Temple of Apollo at Thermon dates from about 630 B.C. It is not the first Doric temple, but it is one of the earliest buildings for which considerable architectural evidence remains. Its long, rectangular plan

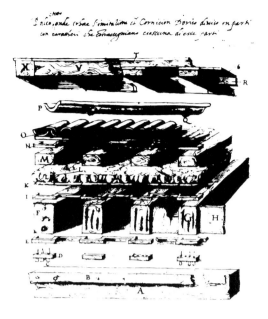

1.6. Gherardo Spini, hypothetical proposal for the wooden antecedent of the Doric entablature from a mid-sixteenth-century manuscript, "I Tre Primi Libri Sopra l'Istritzione de' Greci et Latini Architettori." (Biblioteca Nazionale Marciana di Venezia, Ms. It. IV 38, 5543.)

1.7. William Chambers, "The Third Sort of Huts which gave birth to the Doric Order," from *Civil Architecture*, 1791.

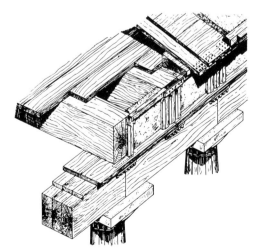

1.8. A. Von Gerkan, hypothetical proposal for the wooden antecedent of the Doric entablature, 1948-49.

1.9. Temple of Apollo at Thermon, c. 630 B.C., plan. (Redrawn by Eric Doud from *Ephemeris Archaeologia*.)

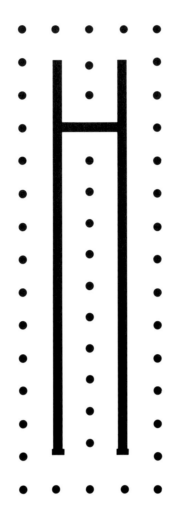

1.10. Temple of Apollo at Thermon, fragment of terra-cotta metope depicting Chelidon, c. 630 B.C. (National Archaeological Museum, Athens, Hirmer Verlag München.)

is indicated by the foundations that were laid for the mud brick walls of its cella and by the stone bases that mark the location and diameter of its wooden columns (fig. 1.9).[10] The foundation is the only structural element that remains. The wooden columns, architraves, and beams were destroyed when the temple was burned by Philip V of Macedonia about 400 years after its erection. The primary clues to the three-dimensional reconstruction of this building come from its decorative clay roof tiles and a set of painted terra-cotta metopes that have survived.

One metope from Thermon depicts the profile of a woman with the word *Chelidon* inscribed above her head (fig. 1.10). Classicists translate this as *Swallow,* the name of a mute princess who killed her nephew, Itys, and prepared the boy's flesh for his unwitting father's supper.[11] This may have been one of several metopes depicting the entire myth. Other panels that survive suggest the story of Perseus and additional cycles. The metope depicting a hideous Gorgon, like the sphinxes on the roof, may have served to ward off evil spirits. Vitruvius assumed that the Doric elements were the product of utilitarian concerns, worked out laboriously with a wholly architectural aim. The psychological and religious motivations behind these terra cottas, however, suggest that their builders responded to more immediate concerns in erecting their temples. Recent scholarship indicates the basic forms of the Doric order were synthesized by a few individuals during an accelerated period of cultural development.[12]

My reconstruction of the Temple of Apollo at Thermon depicts the complex about 500 B.C. (fig. 1.11). The site is thronged with worshippers and priests engaged in the activities of a major religious

center. The sacrificial altar stands before the temple, and the central row of columns obscures the cult statues from direct view. The antae are covered with warriors' shields offered to the deity as ex-votos. The vivid color and ungainly proportions of the temple should kindle interest in it as a predecessor of the more familiar images of Doric architecture. I hope that it will be the first of many attempts to recreate the spirit and sense of place of Thermon and other archaic sites so that we can gain a better appreciation of the Doric order and its origins.

No matter what theory one favors regarding Doric genesis, the evidence of archaeology, even when scanty, must be considered. We are neither limited to what

beliefs Vitruvius inherited from his Hellenistic resources nor to the antiquities that were at hand for Renaissance architects to study. Recent archaeological findings provide insight into architectural problems and are as valuable as the high-tech wizardry that is said to typify our age.

FOUR ROMAN BAROQUE BUILDINGS AND THE TRADITION OF TREATISES: THE MEDIA FOR LEARNING CLASSICAL ARCHITECTURE

Historical buildings are the major resource for learning to design classical architecture. Four buildings in Rome from about 1560 through 1670, helped me learn a canon of proportions for the orders and a system of

1.11. Temple of Apollo at Thermon, watercolor reconstruction by Thomas Gordon Smith, 1986. Perspective view from south.

articulating them in buildings.[13] The details of the Porta Pia, the Palazzo dei Conservatori, Santa Susanna, and Sant' Andrea al Quirinale reveal a rigorous method of thinking about the hierarchical relationships of the orders developed successively by Michelangelo, Maderno, Borromini, and Bernini. Each architect learned the rudiments of this system by looking at the buildings of his predecessors. None of them wrote treatises, but one can understand their intentions by studying the buildings to interpret a theory of the Roman baroque. The photographs of these buildings illustrate how materials, details, and architectural motifs were refined to convey ideas about hierarchy, character and order (figs. 1.12-1.22).

Two structures designed at the end of Michelangelo's life established a vocabulary of compositional themes. The dominant hierarchy of the Porta Pia is based on axial symmetry (fig. 1.12). The central tower was completed only in the mid-nineteenth century, but the enormous scale of the travertine portal draws attention to the center. This ostentation is intensified by the brick material and stark detail of the flanking walls. The string course below the pediment reinforces the contrast by changing from a flat fillet to a fully developed bed mold under the portal cornice (fig. 1.13).

This method of articulation is the basis for Carlo Maderno's 1603 church of Santa Susanna (fig. 1.14). The travertine portion culminates a long development in church facades with superposed orders. They emphasize a symmetrical axis by graduating from pilasters, to engaged columns, to columns only partially connected to the wall. This crescendo is amplified by the flanking brick walls. Four severe pilaster strips emerge from these walls and correspond to the adjacent Corinthian order.

1.12. Michelangelo, Porta Pia, facade, Rome, 1561-64.

1.13. Michelangelo, Porta Pia, detail of pediment of portal and bed mold/string course.

1.14. Carlo Maderno,
Santa Susanna, facade,
Rome, 1603.

1.15. Carlo Maderno,
Santa Susanna, detail of
Corinthian engaged
column, pier and entab-
lature with brick order
to the right.

Although the strips lack capitals, they are connected by a panel at the astragal line to establish horizontal continuity across the entire facade. The junction between travertine and brick at the entablature resembles the contrast seen at the Porta Pia (fig. 1.15). The articulate profiles in travertine are contracted and merged when reduced to brick to emphasize the distinction of hierarchy.

This idea is employed in Francesco Borromini's facade for the Oratorio dei Filippini, 1637-44 (fig. 1.16). The oratory is appended to the travertine facade of Faustino Rughesi's Santa Maria in Vallicella, and Borromini thought of his building in relation to the brick flanks at Santa Susanna

1.16. Francesco Bor-
romini, Oratorio dei
Filippini, Rome,
1637-44. Detail of
stripped-down Corin-
thian order adjacent to
Fausto Rughesi's facade
of Santa Maria in Val-
licella, 1593-1606.

(fig. 1.34). Like Maderno, he chose brick
and simplified the pilaster capitals and
entablature that correspond to Rughesi's
conventional order. The cornice that links
the two facades is rendered with the same
abbreviated profile as Santa Susanna.

Michelangelo's second type of hierarchical planning was developed in the Palazzo
dei Conservatori on the Campidoglio in
Rome. Although it may have been planned
about 1540, only two bays were erected by
the time of Michelangelo's death. Construction of the mirror image Palazzo Nuovo was
only begun in 1603 and was completed by
the 1660s. It must have provided an ongoing paradigm for baroque architects (fig.
1.17). The development of Corinthian
pilasters superimposed upon sturdy piers
form the bays of a giant order which
dominates the smaller Ionic columns of the
portico (figs. 1.18, 1.19). This hierarchical
system is striated rather than axial. The
composition of the bay has precedents in
Bramante and Raphael, but the idea had
never been so dramatically expressed.

1.17. Michelangelo, Palazzo Nuovo, facade, Rome, executed between 1603 and the 1660s.

1.18. Michelangelo, Palazzo Nuovo, detail of pilaster pedestal and Ionic order.

1.19. Michelangelo, Palazzo Nuovo, detail of Ionic capital and entablature.

1.20. Gian Lorenzo Bernini, Sant' Andrea al Quirinale facade, Rome, 1657-72.

1.21. Gian Lorenzo Bernini, Sant' Andrea al Quirinale, elevation of Campidoglio motif.

1.22. Gian Lorenzo Bernini, Sant' Andrea al Quirinale, detail of Ionic capital and entablature in travertine and brick.

The composition of the Campidoglio palazzi was employed throughout the baroque and neoclassical periods. Its influence is evident in Borromini's facade of San Carlo alle Quattro Fontane (fig. 1.5). Its most intelligent employment is in Gian Lorenzo Bernini's Sant' Andrea al Quirinale in Rome (fig. 1.20). The church was begun in 1657, but the facade was not crystalized until 1667 and the portico was added as a final gesture only in 1670. The elevation consists of a single pedimented bay from the Campidoglio enframing a minor Ionic order of pilasters that flank the portal (fig. 1.21). Bernini must have felt that this was not dramatic enough and carried freestanding columns out to support the overhang of the Ionic entablature. A magnificent escutcheon and curved raking cornice are perched on the edge of the portico roof threatening imbalance.

Bernini broke the relatively two-dimensional mold of the Campidoglio motif not only in the portico. He also combined this motif with the "crescendo" theme from the Porta Pia and Santa Susanna by continuing the Ionic entablature behind the pier and exposing it on the convex brick walls of the chapel as the reduced profile supported by brick pilaster strips (fig. 1.22). This example of how a tradition was synthesized and refined in one building at the end of the high baroque period demonstrates the rich potential for experimentation while conforming to an architectural tradition.

The treatise is a complementary resource for learning classical architecture. One type is the graphic catalogue of details such as the *Codex Coner,* compiled in the early 1500s.[14] It consists of wash drawings of ancient and Renaissance buildings and architectural fragments. It was never published in book form, but the manuscript was

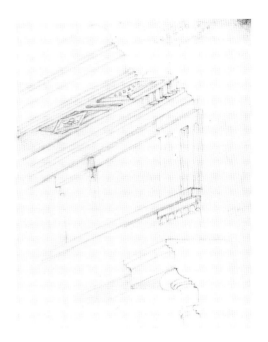

1.24. Francesco Borromini, sketch of a Doric entablature. Based on drawing no. 102 in the *Codex Coner,* c. 1500. (Reproduced from Ashby's text, *Sixteenth Century Drawings.*)

available to architects. Michelangelo copied the Doric order of the Theater of Marcellus from it (fig. 1.23).[15] More than 100 years later Borromini sketched another Doric entablature from the *Codex* and employed its unusual triglyphs in his aediculae at the Palazzo della Propaganda Fide (fig. 1.24, 3.13).[16] Contemporary architects should emulate this practice by sketching details from historical buildings and utilize their notebooks when solving problems in design.

The architectural treatise is the most formal medium for transmitting the literary and graphic information of classical architecture. Although the books of

Vitruvius, Alberti, Palladio, Perrault, Laugier, and Chambers vary in intent, they all develop components of what could be called a canonical treatise.[17] First, they contain didactic regulations on the proportions of the orders and typological patterns for their articulation in buildings. Second, they present a theoretical approach to the practice of classical architecture and stimulate vitality in building. Third, they use historical buildings as models for emulation and to support the theoretical intent. Finally, in the case of practicing architects such as Vitruvius, Palladio, or Chambers, the author illustrates his own buildings to demonstrate the vigor of the tradition.

The *Ten Books on Architecture,* by the first-century B.C. Roman architect Vitruvius Pollio, includes the components just enumerated: canon, theory, historical examples, and a presentation of his own work. In addition to these architectural subjects, he adds commentary on music, building materials, weather, and even theories of national temperament.[18] Although Vitruvius's range of subjects may be too digressive, his book underlines the concept that classical architecture relates to many disciplines.

No ancient manuscripts of Vitruvius's treatise exist. He refers to ten illustrations in the text, but none of them survive even in copied form.[19] The earliest copy dates from the ninth century, and its survival is probably due to the renewed interest in ancient literature promoted by the emperor Charlemagne and the preservation of this material in monastic libraries.[20]

While Vitruvius's work is the only treatise to be preserved from antiquity, it was not unique in the ancient world. He complains of a dearth of similar books in his own period but he apparently borrowed heavily from a well-established tradition of architectural writings. He lists the names of thirteen Greek authors, but no books by these men have come to light.[21] Pytheos and Hermogenes are cited frequently and we are told that they wrote about their buildings, which survive in ruins at Priene, Teos, and Magnesia.[22] Perhaps one day someone will find Hermogenes' text on the linen wrapping of a mummy or in a bookcase in Alexandria. That discovery would undoubtedly change and enrich our view of classical architecture. Until then, we can only speculate on Vitruvius's debt to his sources from his statement, "From their commentaries I have gathered what I saw was useful for the present subject, and formed it into one complete treatise."[23]

We think of Vitruvius as a Roman architect, but he was espousing an aesthetic formulated in buildings constructed between 100 and 300 years before his own time. He was striving to revive Hellenistic canons in a Roman world moving headlong into new volumetric architectural forms made possible with materials like concrete. We do not know how influential Vitruvius was in his lifetime, but if he was ignored in antiquity, he has been exalted subsequently. Because of the authority he has held since the Renaissance, Hellenistic models have had an overriding impact on our perception and evaluation of classical architecture.

Bramante and Raphael were the first Renaissance architects to assimilate Vitruvius's text. Through building they began to resolve it with their understanding of Roman archaeology.[24] Relying on their precedent, Palladio reinstated the Vitruvian ideal in his buildings, and in *Quattro Libri di Architettura* he drew the Tuscan and Doric orders directly from Vitruvius.[25] Although his books incorporate much original material, the *Quattro*

Libri disseminated Hellenistic proportions throughout the world and the influence of this system continues today. In his buildings Palladio used the configurations of Vitruvius's trabeated peripteral temples; the hexastyle Ionic portico of the Villa Foscari at Mira is an exquisite example (figs. 1.25, 1.26).

In 1556 Palladio provided drawings and influenced the commentary of Daniele Barbaro's authoritative translation of Vitruvius.[26] Fourteen years later, Palladio wrote his own treatise. If he borrowed freely from Vitruvius's canon, why did he have to write a new one at all? In 1673 Claude Perrault published his translation of Vitruvius.[27] A decade later he wrote his *Ordonnance* to promote his own opinion on similar issues. Was Vitruvius's authority not convincing in the sixteenth or seventeenth century?

There are many functional problems in Vitruvius's text—ambiguous passages and incomplete prescriptions. These editorial and interpretive problems were not what motivated Palladio and Perrault to the task of writing their own books. The answer lies in the polemical nature of the treatise.

Alberti, Palladio, Perrault, Laugier, and Chambers all considered classical architecture to be a contemporary medium. By advocating its practice in the context of their own time and place, they had to consider the factors of local tradition, available materials, and weather. They had to grapple with the problems that resulted from trying to execute the ideal standards of Vitruvius with temporal constraints. Palladio built the Vitruvian columns at the Villa Foscari in brick, for example, because stone was not economically available in the Veneto. Because these men believed in their own interpretation of practice, they also confronted a less tangible challenge: they

1.25. Andrea Palladio, Villa Foscari, Mira, c. 1560. Ionic portico facing the Brenta canal.

1.26. Andrea Palladio, Villa Foscari. Interior of Ionic portico.

1.27. Claude Perrault,
pl. I from *Ordonnace
des cinq èspeces de
colonnes,* 1683.

1.28. Guarino Guarini, variations on the Corinthian
order and Solomonic column shafts. Pl. IV from Trat-
tato 3, *Architettura Civile,* plates first published in
1686, published with text in 1737.

disagreed with contemporaries who held conflicting theories of how buildings should be formed, and their books were written to set things straight in an atmosphere of controversy. Classicism was dominant in France when Perrault wrote his treatise, but architects at the academy of Louis XIV were arguing bitterly over the fine points of theory and proportion. Perrault sought to prescribe a canon upon which all would agree (fig. 1.27)! The thirty pages of his preface succeeded only in stimulating greater debate, and even today, reading this section should keep architects at the edge of their seats.[28]

Laugier's *Essai* is an adamant polemic against the baroque sensibility. The conservative Chambers not only blasted the

baroque but railed against the up-and-coming Stuart and Revett, who challenged his Roman models with the newly rediscovered paradigm of Greek architecture.[29] These examples of classicists arguing with classicists are the most common stimuli for treatise writing, and this type of agreement might even have been the impetus for Vitruvius.

At other times classicists find themselves in conflict with alien aesthetic views. In the 1400s, Alberti fought the Gothic mentality in himself in his search for classicism. In the 1500s, Palladio created his architecture in the essentially Gothic milieu of the Veneto.[30] In the 1600s, Guarino Guarini threatened the limits of classicism with his openness to Gothic sensibility and exalted

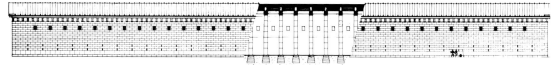

the varied and bizarre in an approach radically different from his contemporary, Perrault (fig.1.28).

All of these architect–authors, often considered names in a morgue of dusty academic volumes, were radical figures. Despite divergent points of view, they challenged the overbearing dogmatism that is an unfortunate misinterpretation of the principle of rule in the classical system. These architects did not want to destroy rule, as did the authors of the disintegrating DADA manifestos of the early twentieth century; they wanted to substitute an alternate standard for old models that had become moribund. By the nature of their efforts, they were receptive to invention. No matter how polemical Laugier seems, his goal is the reconstruction of radical principles and authentic forms. The same is true for Palladio, Perrault, and even Chambers. They might violently disagree on what the forms should look like, but their aim is constructive. This characteristic brings their books to life and makes their architecture authentic.

PHILO'S ARSENAL: THE SOLUTION OF FUNCTIONAL PROBLEMS

The Arsenal of the Athenian Navy was designed by the architect Philo of Eleusis and built between 347 and 326 B.C. in Peiraeus.[31] The structure was destroyed without trace, along with all Athenian fortifications, 250 years later by the Roman conquerer Sulla. The form of the building can be reconstructed by piecing together information from an inscribed marble slab

found by archaeologists in 1882. It presents specifications for the contractor and public overseers. Since its discovery, numerous reconstructions have been made. They agree in general configuration, but vary in detail due to phrases that are difficult to interpret.

As one would expect for a building of its time, the scheme is modular and rational (fig. 1.29). Although the Arsenal was for storage and defense, Philo did not limit his criteria to functionalism and therefore build the Athenian equiavalent of a "Butler" prefabricated warehouse. Instead, the Arsenal was constructed of limestone ashlar blocks with door jambs of Pentelic marble. A triglyph and metope frieze supported a cornice with pediments at each end of the gabled roof. This imposing building both solved practical problems and communicated attitudes of civic pride to reinforce impressions of military strength. The Arsenal was conceived as a work of art and display as well as function.

Like all great classical architects, Philo was responsive to many factors. Within the limits of budget and purpose, he emulated the monumental Athenian buildings of the previous century, such as the prostyle Temple of the Athenians at Delos (fig. 3.10).[32] Philo may have also been influenced by written treatises, and, although it does not survive, according to Vitruvius, he wrote one himself about the Arsenal and the proportions of temples. Finally, Philo had to express the pride and fulfill the wishes not only of the admirals, but of the citizens of Athens, whose financial support was essential for its con-

1.29. Philo of Eleusis, Arsenal for the Athenian Navy, Peiraeus, 347-326 B.C. (Reconstruction of elevations by John Tittmann.)

1.30. Donato Bramante, rendered elevation of San Pietro in Montorio, Rome, c. 1502. (Sopraintendenza alle Galerie per le Provincie di Firenze, Uffizi, Arch 135,68851.)

1.31. Donato Bramante, Doric peristyle, San Pietro in Montorio.

struction. Perhaps its success as a symbol of military strength was one factor that made the Arsenal a target for Sulla's marauding troops in 87-86 B.C.[33]

BRAMANTE'S SAN PIETRO IN MONTORIO: SCULPTURE AND IDEAS

In Philo's Arsenal, functional problems were essential but not preeminent. On the other hand, some buildings have a primarily monumental function, and the architect must concentrate on problems of sculpture and significance. In about 1502, Donato Bramante created the Tempietto in the cloister of San Pietro in Montorio, Rome. Ferdinando and Isabella of Spain initiated the project and a Spanish cardinal oversaw its progress. The Tempietto was the first fully classical building of the Roman Renaissance, and the enthusiasm of an experiment

must have surrounded its design and construction (fig. 1.30).[34]

The chapel commemorates the spot where Renaissance theologians thought St. Peter was crucified. Bramante encircled the place of crucifixion with a centralized chapel. As an architect–archaeologist, he had gained a practical understanding of Roman buildings, and San Pietro is the fruit of his studies. He extended the Vitruvian tradition that ascribed an order to the character of a deity to a Christian saint. Peter is one of the more virile saints in the Christian pantheon, and Bramante chose the Doric order, traditionally ascribed to Hercules, to convey Peter's heroic status.[35]

Bramante set himself a difficult task by selecting the Doric. Although this order conveys a sense of strength and simplicity, it is the most complex to use because the modular frieze does not permit flexible spacing of columns in a peristyle. For economy, Renaissance architects routinely used column shafts from despoiled ancient structures, and the sixteen monolithic granite shafts at San Pietro are examples of this practice. Bramante solved the spacing puzzle of the peristyle and resolved the larger sculptural problems of the building by allowing the arbitrary module of the columns to create a proportional system for a building that combined a Renaissance dome with the Vitruvian circular temple (fig. 1.31).[36]

Another aspect of the Tempietto demonstrates Bramante's capacity to use classical architecture in a narrative way. In the sober Doric order figural imagery is confined to the metopes. Bramante treated the frieze with an iconography parallel to ancient tradition. He must have known examples of Roman metopes in which the sculpted skull of an ox, or boukranion, was used to decorate the Doric order (fig. 1.32). This symbol of blood sacrifice in pagan worship commemorates a presumed practice in archaic Doric temples in which the head of a sacrificed animal would be affixed to the entablature and bleached by the sun.[37] In the Hellenistic period this *momento mori* was incorporated into the sculptural program of Doric structures. Ritually-painted animal skulls have been found in non-Egyptian grave sites along the Nile, and they date at least 1,000 years before their use in Greece (fig. 1.33).[38] Bramante adapted this primordial idea by sculpting parallel symbols of Christian sacrifice, like the chalice and Eucharist, in the metopes at San Pietro.

Despite the inherent limitations of architectural elements to transmit literal ideas, Bramante developed both the sculptural and pictorial forms of San Pietro in Montorio to make statements that reinforce the meaning and impact of its sacred place.

1.32. Fragment of a Roman Doric entablature with sculpted boukranion in the Museo Nazionale Romano, Rome.

1.33. Painted ox skull found in a non-Egyptian grave deposit in mid-Egypt, 1786-1570 B.C. (The Metropolitan Museum of Art, Rogers Fund, 1915, 16.2.23.)

1.34. Francesco Borromini, Oratorio dei Filippini, facade, 1637-44. A photographic montage mirrors the building to illustrate Borromini's intent to flank Fausto Rughesi's facade of Santa Maria in Vallicella with two brick dependencies by proposing a new facade for a "Pamphilj Pantheon" in 1644.

BORROMINI'S ORATORIO DEI FILIPPINI: THE CLIENT WHO SHARES THE CLASSICAL VISION

The architect's intent to make classical buildings will remain only a dream unless clients provide the moral and financial backing to see a vision become reality. The client can take many forms. Philo is said to have delivered a persuasive speech that galvanized civic support to erect his Arsenal.[39] The sanctuary at Thermon was erected with contributions from people who came from points all around the Mediterranean to supplicate Apollo. Since classical buildings are generally monumental and civic in nature, they require the broad financial support of the populace. Although this burden is borne by many, there is usually one official who has the vision to patronize a particular architect and to see the building to completion.

Despite the wide base of support required, the selection of ideas that a building will state through architectural forms is not a collective decision. These intentions are specialized and demand a corporate spokesman who has a keen interest in architecture. The records of such clients are scanty, but one assumes that many projects have been realized due to their involvement.

One documented example is the construction, beginning in 1637, of Borromini's Oratorio dei Filippini. In his monograph *Borromini and the Roman Oratory,* Joseph Connors presents the relationship between architect, patron, and corporate client with unusual candor.[40] He credits the oratorian Padre Virgilio Spada as a persuasive client who introduced the relatively unknown Borromini to the confraternity of priests. Spada had an amateur's passion for architecture, and beyond securing financial backing for construction, he undoubtedly served as a critic during the process of design. Spada acted as Borromini's apologist for the confraternity; later he was ghost writer for Borromini's treatise, *Opus Architectonicum.*[41] This book presented the designs for the Oratorio and pleaded for a rational critique of his solutions. As Connors and the tone of the *Opus* indicate, Borromini's first major monument would not have been built without the support of his intercessor, Virgilio Spada.

Later a different client proposed a project (which remained visionary) for the Oratory and its adjacent church, Santa Maria in Vallicella. Connors writes:

> *During the first few months of Innocent X's papacy in 1644 there was hope for a new commission at the Vallicella which would have allowed Borromini to integrate the Oratory facade into a larger and more satisfying context. He was asked to design a monumental Pamphili Chapel along the right flank of the church . . . he turned to antiquity and proposed a mausoleum drawn from Montano's engravings. The whole complex was conceived as a pendant to the casa, and it was given a facade that would have reflected the Oratory facade in mirror symmetry. Everything that had characterized the original . . . found its way into the duplicate. If built it would have been part of a triple facade, the ultimate baroque expression of the idea of controlled context that had its modest beginnings in the brick walls flanking the facade of . . . Santa Susanna.*[42]

Unfortunately, Pope Innocent X did not build this project, but a photographic montage interprets Connors's reading of Borromini's sketchy plan of the complex (figs. 1.16, 1.34, 1.35).

All of the historical buildings, drawings and treatises presented demonstrate the factors that must be integrated to revive classical architecture today. Chapter 2 provides the material necessary to begin this process. It presents objective canons for the orders and illustrates how they can be employed to articulate buildings. This tangible point of reference for learning the forms and systems of classical architecture is the basis of rule and should stimulate invention.

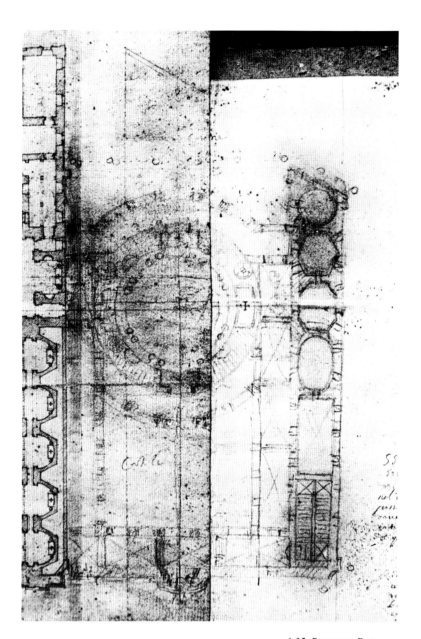

1.35. Francesco Borromini, Oratorio dei Filippini. Partial plan of Oratory, Santa Maria in Vallicella and the "Pamphilj Pantheon," proposed in 1644. (Collection of the Albertina, Vienna, no. 285.)

THE ORDERS—FROM SUBSTANCE TO EBULLIENCE

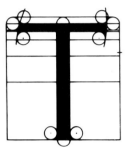

THE ORDERS ARE PRESENTED IN THIS CHAPTER emphasizing the capacity of classical architecture to be expressive by differentiating character (fig. 2.1). Throughout history there has been a natural interpollination between the orders; the Doric echinus, for example, has occasionally been carved with the egg and dart motif, properly an Ionic element. This practice contradicts the expression of character and should be avoided.

Each order is presented here in a simple format: a pair of columns supports an entablature, and additional drawings show measurements and details. Developing a canon is a reductive act. The object is to fabricate the "perfect" Doric order. Although it is a theoretical exercise and practice will force these standards to be somewhat flexible, the canon is vital to architectural practice because it defines a standard point of reference.

THE GENERIC RELATIONSHIPS OF THE ORDERS

The unit of measurement used to construct the orders is the module based upon the diameter of a column shaft. This modular unit is divided or multiplied to produce ratios that determine the measurements of other components and regulate the proportions. The height of a column is determined by easily-remembered ratios. For instance, the Doric is 1:7.5. Ratios for the distance between columns determine the width of the building, and this can be multiplied to determine its large-scale dimensions. Meticulous ratios govern the subdivisions of the entablature and details of the capital and base. These ratios are given in decimals of the modular unit and can be easily computed on the calculator for use with either metric or English systems of measurement.

2.1 The five orders articulate a gateway to show their canonical proportions and hierarchical relationships. Each order is equated to a figure that represents its character in anthropomorphic terms.

2.2. Reconstruction of the Etruscan temple according to Vitruvius's *Ten Books,* bk. IV, ch. VII. Rome University, Istituto di Etruscologia e di Antichità Italiche. (Fototeca Unione at the American Academy in Rome, F.U. 14427F.)

THE TUSCAN ORDER: THE REPRESENTATION OF SUBSTANCE

The Tuscan is Italic, not Greek, in origin. It is the most rudimentary order in form and character. Its column is squat, its entablature is low, and the overhang of its roof is broad. The Tuscan architrave is wooden and is doubled to span a wide distance between columns.

The Tuscan order was not practiced in consistent form in ancient times, but Vitruvius reduced its elements to a regular type (fig. 2.2).[2] The information in his *Ten Books* allowed the Tuscan to be revived during the sixteenth century in Italy. Renaissance architects were not interested in its original function as a temple for Etruscan religion; for them its simplicity represented a brusque character appropriate for agricultural and military buildings. Vitruvius's vague description of the complex Tuscan roof structure was ignored by Renaissance architects and has only been better understood thanks to the discovery of elaborate terra cottas used to sheathe the beams and ornament the roof.

The Tuscan order projects a straightforward and unpretentious character and may be employed to enhance the utilitarian portions of a building. James Ackerman has linked it with the intentionally rough appearance of Renaissance rusticated masonry, and this association should be developed.[3] Although compared to the other orders the Tuscan appears awkward, it defines a baseline against which the more refined orders can be seen. Therefore, it is essential to the concept of hierarchy in classical architecture. Because of its solidity it projects a quality of directness and honesty. The Tuscan should be employed with respect for this quality of substance.

The Tuscan order presented here follows the format of Vitruvius, except that the overhang attempts to resolve his description with archaeological findings (figs. 2.3, 2.4, 2.5).

2.3. Tuscan trabeation.

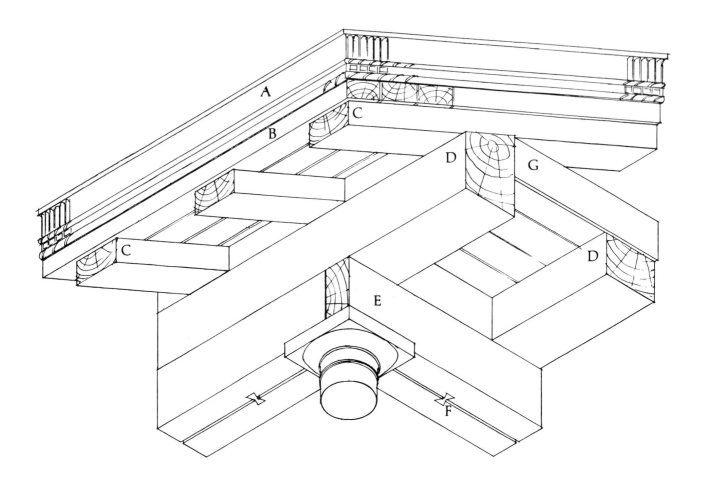

2.4. Tuscan Vocabulary

Entablature
  A. Terra-cotta Sima
  B. Purlin (Templa)
  C. Rafters (Cantherii)
  D. Mutule (Traiecturae mutulorum)
  E. Architrave (Trabes compactiles)
  F. Dovetail Tenon and Mortise
  G. Casing
  H. Column
  I. Capital
    J. Abacus
    K. Echinus
    L. Neck
      M. Fillet
      N. Apophyge
  O. Shaft
    P. Astragal (torus and fillet)
    Q. Apophyge
  R. Base
    S. Fillet
    T. Torus
    U. Cylindrical Plinth
  V. Podium

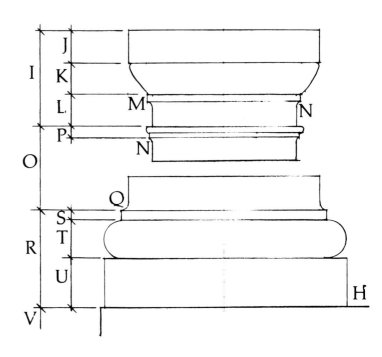

2.5. Tuscan dimensions and method for shaft: Column shafts are cylindrical for the first third of their height and diminish in diameter as they approach the neck. If diminution were equal, the upper portion would be a truncated cone, but the practice of designing the shaft with entasis, a subtly increasing curvature as it ascends, gives the column a lively profile. The method shown in this figure is employed for all orders and is derived from Vignola.

Imagine a half sphere 1m in diameter resting upon the lower third of the column shaft. The remaining two-thirds of the shaft is divided into six equal units. The upper boundary is a disk the diameter of the neck, in the case of the Tuscan .75m. The diameters of the intermediate subdivisions are determined by dropping the neck diameter down to the hemisphere. The arc formed by this intersection is divided into six equal units. Each of these points is raised to a corresponding subdivision to establish a progressively diminishing series of diameters. In elevation, these points are joined into a subtle curving line, the continuous curve of entasis.

2.6. Doric construction and polychromy.

THE DORIC ORDER: THE EXPRESSION OF STRENGTH

The monumental Doric order was developed for temples in mainland Greece and spread throughout the Mediterranean in the 500s B.C. as a result of Greek colonization.

In early temples, robust white columns with simple capitals supported a heavy entablature. The frieze and upper zones were enlivened by the rich polychromy of vivid red, blue, green, and gold. Through the period of the Parthenon in Athens, Doric proportions became more refined and the moldings more taut. By the Hellenistic period, under the influence of Ionic proportions, the order became excessively slim and was close to losing the hallmarks of its traditional character (figs. 3.11, 3.22).

Vitruvius presented this version of the order in a description of a temple with a four-columned portico (fig. 3.5). The earlier versions of the Doric were not known in Europe until the Parthenon and other buildings were published in the late eighteenth century. This sparked ongoing debates between the "Greeks" and "Romans" over fine points, like the position of triglyphs at the corners. These arguments were magnified by arguments over general issues, such as the cultural superiority of the Romans versus the Greeks.

Although the Doric is the second most rudimentary of the orders, its entablature has the most complex geometry of all. It is difficult to comprehend; one must draw its elements in perspective as Michelangelo did to understand how they are combined (figs. 1.23, 2.6).

The Doric order is appropriate for any type of building in which a dignified and sober character should be expressed. It is difficult to design with because the rigid rhythm of its frieze limits the number of possible intercolumniations. The same modules must be anticipated in planning a building with exterior walls, like Philo's Arsenal at Peiraeus, rather than a columnar peristyle. When columns are used they are never on an axial grid because their position is determined by the distribution of the triglyphs.

My presentation of the Doric order moderates between the heavy example of the Parthenon and the refinement of the Hellenistic style (fig. 2.7, 4.1).[4] The coloration reflects the arrangement that seems to have been canonical for the Greeks, although variations were common.[5] Details, such as the slopes of the mutule and the co-planar relationship of the architrave and triglyph, are reinstated from the Hellenic tradition in order to give maximum credibility to the representational role of these elements and greater authenticity to the order (figs. 2.7-2.9).

2.7. Doric trabeation.

2.8. Doric Vocabulary
A. Entablature
  B. Cornice
    C. Cavetto Sima
    D. Corona
      E. Fillet
      F. Apophyge
    G. Mutule with guttae
    H. Via(e) with Drip
    I. Frieze cap (bed mold)
  J. Frieze
    K. Triglyph
      L. Femur
      M. Glyph (channel)
      N. Semiglyph
    O. Metope
      P. Boukranion
      Q. Patera
  R. Architrave
    S. Taenia
    T. Regula
    U. Guttae
    V. Fascia
W. Column
  X. Capital
    Y. Abacus
    Z. Echinus
    AA. Neck
      BB. Annulets
      CC. Sinking groove
  DD. Shaft
    EE. Flute
    FF. Arris
  GG. Stylobate
  HH. Anta capital
    II. Hawk's beak
    JJ. Cyma reversa
KK. Pediment of distyle in
antis temple front
  LL. Raking cornice
  MM. Split fillet
  NN. Tympanum
  OO. Akroterion
PP. Anta
QQ. Crepidoma
RR. Intercolumniation

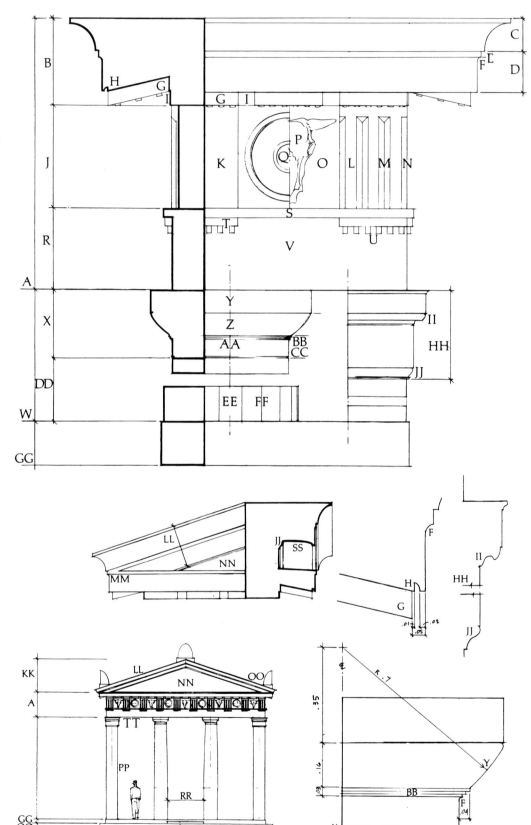

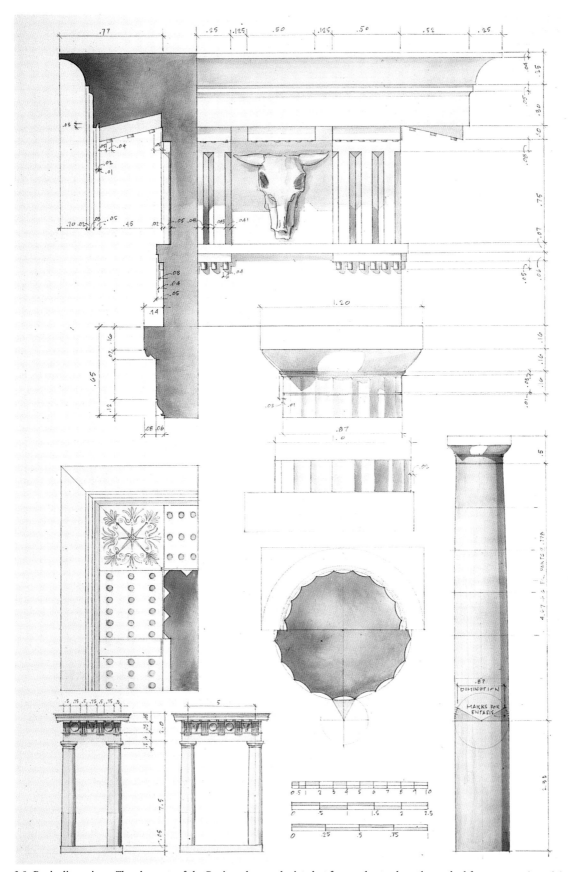

2.9. Doric dimensions. The elements of the Doric order are depicted at four scales to show the method for construction of detail.

2.10. Ionic capital, portion of shaft and base, Temple of Artemis, Sardis, c. 325 B.C. (The Metropolitan Museum of Art, gift of the American Society for the Exploration of Sardis, 1926, 26.59.1.)

THE IONIC ORDER: THE ARTICULATION OF REFINEMENT

Some of the ancient architects said that the Doric order ought not to be used for temples, because faults and incongruities were caused by the laws of its symmetry. Arcesius and Pytheos said so, as well as Hermogenes. He, for instance, after getting together a supply of marble for the construction of a Doric temple, changed his mind and built an Ionic temple to Father Bacchus with the same materials. This is not because it is unlovely in appearance or origin or dignity of form, but because the arrangement of the triglyphs and metopes is an embarrassment and inconvenience to the work.

VITRUVIUS, IV, III[6]

The Ionic order is ambiguous in character. It is traditionally associated with matronly female or scholarly male subjects. Its delicate moldings are sensuous in comparison to the severe Doric, while the harmonious rhythm of its columns is produced by a rationally planned grid. Its impalpable capital is its most characteristic feature. All classical capitals distribute the load of a rectilinear architrave to a cylindrical column shaft, but the Ionic emphasizes this structural function with a piece of sinuous sculpture. The Ionic order should be used when a median between the seriousness of the Doric and the delicacy of the Corinthian is desired.

The earliest monumental capitals were produced in Asia Minor about 550 B.C.[7] At the Temple of Hera on Samos a stone echinus carved with egg and dart survives; archaeologists speculate that a wooden volute and abacus surmounted this. Fragments of capitals from the Temple of Artemis at Ephesus combine the echinus and volutes in one piece.[8]

A much later capital from the Temple of Artemis at Sardis is embellished with

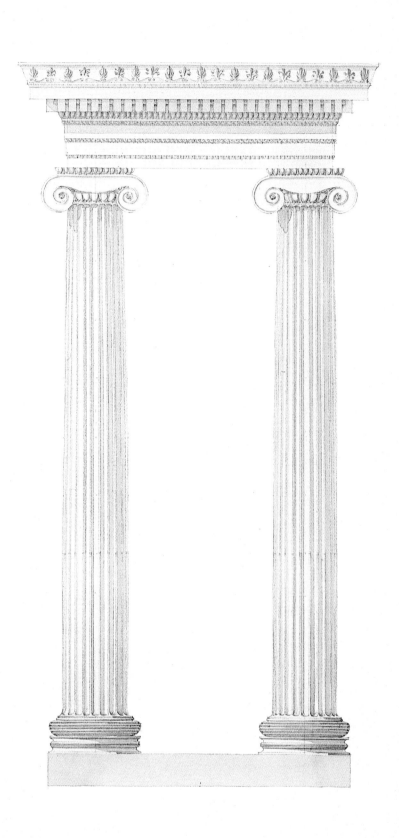

2.11. Ionic trabeation.

Corinthian-style acanthus, but otherwise it is a good demonstration of the Ionic form (fig. 2.10).[9] Two volutes are joined by a horizontal canalis to form a symmetrical face. These occur both on the front and back of the capital (fig. 2.12). The faces are bound together by bolsters on either side (fig. 2.13). The bolsters can be conceived as taut, elastic membranes attached to the rigid perimeter of each volute. Between the volutes they contract toward the neck of the column. They must not contract too tightly, however, or they obscure the twenty-four units of egg and dart carved into the echinus. The separation between the echinus and volute at Samos should be recalled. Although the bolster contracts on the underside, its upper portion hangs in flaccid manner. Michelangelo carries this quality to an extreme in his Ionic capitals at the Campidoglio (fig. 2.14).

The bolster of the Sardis capital is articulated with double roundels and embellished with palmettes, an Ionic motif. The bead and reel below the echinus, and the egg and tongue of the abacus, are both considered Ionic moldings. A cyma reversa carved with the Lesbian leaf motif (from the island of Lesbos) is the alternate embellishment for the abacus (fig. 2.21).

2.12. Details of Sardis capital showing the influence of the Corinthian order in the elaborately wrought acanthus embellishments. (The Metropolitan Museum of Art, gift of the American Society for the Exploration of Sardis, 1926, 26.59.1.)

2.13. Three-quarter view of Sardis capital showing the volute and bolster sides. (The Metropolitan Museum of Art, gift of the American Society for the Exploration of Sardis, 1926, 26.59.1.)

2.14. Michelangelo, Palazzo Nuovo, detail of Ionic capital, designed 1564, executed between 1603 and the 1660s.

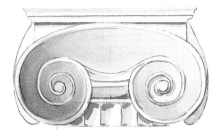

2.15. Three-faceted Ionic capital, Temple of Apollo, Bassae, 430-400 B.C. (Drawn from Cockerell.)
2.16. Scamozzi "Ionic" capital. (Drawn from Vincenzo Scamozzi, *Dell' Idea dell' Architettura Universale*.)
2.17. Composite capital. (Drawn from Vignola's *Regola dei cinque ordini*.)
2.18. Aeolic capital. (Drawn from Scully's publication of Klopedi in *The Earth, the Temple and the Gods*.)

The frontal nature of the Ionic capital presents a problem at the corner of a peristyle. In order to face the columns outward at the flank, the corner capital must have two faces perpendicular to each other on the outside and two bolsters inside. Iktinos ingeniously solved this problem at the Temple of Apollo at Bassae (fig. 2.15).[10] He made the front volute tangent with two half volutes at the diagonal. The use of this form on all four sides of the capital allows it to serve either an exterior or a re-entrant corner situation.

The Scamozzi capital has this flexibility also, but it is not a worthy substitute for the Ionic (fig. 2.16). It is an abbreviation of the Composite capital with four volutes that spring on the diagonal from the echinus (fig. 2.17). The volutes deny a primary characteristic of the Ionic because they are not connected to each other. The Scamozzi capital resembles the Aeolic capitals of Palestine composed of two volutes that spring from the column shaft and curve up like the horns of a goat (fig. 2.18).[11]

2.19. Ionic dimensions. The elements of the Ionic order are depicted at four scales to show the method for construction of detail.

The Samian (fig. 2.19) and Ephesian (fig. 2.22) types of column bases characterize the Ionic order and originate from the archaic temples mentioned earlier.[12] They are composed of two moldings; a convex torus rests upon a concave spira. The Attic base of the Corinthian order is often used for the Ionic but it does not reinforce the Ionic character.

The order shown here revives a number of early characteristics of the Ionic. The volutes of the capital are widely spaced and their faces incline slightly downward. The base reinstates the prototype from Asia Minor, and the entablature has no frieze (figs. 2.18-2.21).

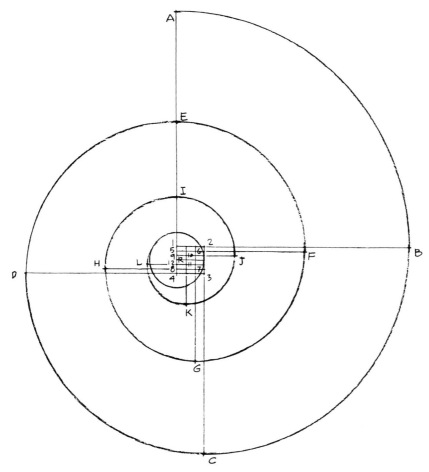

The method for constructing the spiral of the Ionic volute is based on the engraving and description published by William Chambers in 1791 as *Goldman's Volute*. This version incorporates several reinterpretations by Terrance O'Neil that clarify the method for creating the reducing fillet of the spiral.

After determining the radius point R of the eye from the dimensions provided, inscribe the eye with a radius of 0.037m and draw the cathetus, the vertical axis AR. Construct a square with sides of 0.037m originating on this vertical axis with the outer vertical tangent to the eye. The square is centered on the horizontal axis from R. Divide the vertical sides into six equal lengths (1.006) and the horizontal sides into three equal segments (.012). Connect these points to form a grid as seen in detail R, figure 2.20. Define three squares all colinear with the cathetus. The outer, with points 1, 2, 3, 4 is the full dimension of 0.037m. The second is numbered 5, 6, 7, 8, and the innermost is 9, 10, 11, 12. This succession defines the radius points for drawing the spiral with a compass.

To begin the spiral, place the point of the compass on 1, extend the arm to A and swing an arc to B. Next, move the compass point to 2 and form the arc BC. Proceed to 3 for the arc CD, and continue around the squares until reaching radius point 12, whose arc should become tangent to the eye.

To create a second spiral that produces a fillet that reduces in width as it approaches the eye, a smaller series of boxes must be drawn superimposed on the first. The largest of these squares is 0.034m, as shown in detail S, figure 2.20. Its dimension is determined by drawing a right angle triangle consisting of the cathetus, a perpendicular segment AZ measuring 0.0185m, or 0.037m ÷ 2, and hypotenuse RZ. When a line is drawn perpendicular to the cathetus from A^1, its intersection with RZ produces Z_1. A_1Z_1 is 0.017m in length. This is multiplied by 2 to determine the dimensions of the second set of radius squares. The same procedure is followed for determining the points 1_1-12_1, and arcs swung from this succession of points will produce a second spiral that gradually tapers as it "parallels" the first.

2.20 and 2.21. Ionic
Vocabulary and
Dimensions
Capital
A. Abacus, cyma reversa
carved with lesbian leaf
B. Volute
    C. Spiral molding
    D. Canalis
    E. Eye
    F. Bolster or
pulvinus
    G. Balteus
    H. Palmette
    I. Echinus
Column Shaft
J. Astragal carved with
bead and reel
    K. Fillet
    L. Apophyge
M. Column neck
    N. Apophyge
    O. Astragal
Column Base
P. Torus carved with
horizontal flutes
Q. Ephesian spira
R. Subdivision of square
to determine radii of
primary volute spiral
S. Subdivision of smaller
square to determine
radii for reducing mold-
ing of spiral.
T. Entablature
    U. Cornice
        V. Cyma recta
Sima carved with anthe-
mion pattern of lotus
and palmette
        W. Corona with
cyma reversa carved
with Lesbian leaf motif
        X. Cyma reversa
and Ionic soffit
        Y. Dentil course
        Z. Ovolo carved
with egg and tongue
    AA. Architrave
        BB. Cyma reversa
        CC. Fascia
        DD. Cyma reversa
EE. Anta capital
    FF. Abacus
    GG. Cymation carved
with egg and tongue
    HH. Anthemion motif
    II. Astragal with
bead and reel
    JJ. Shaft

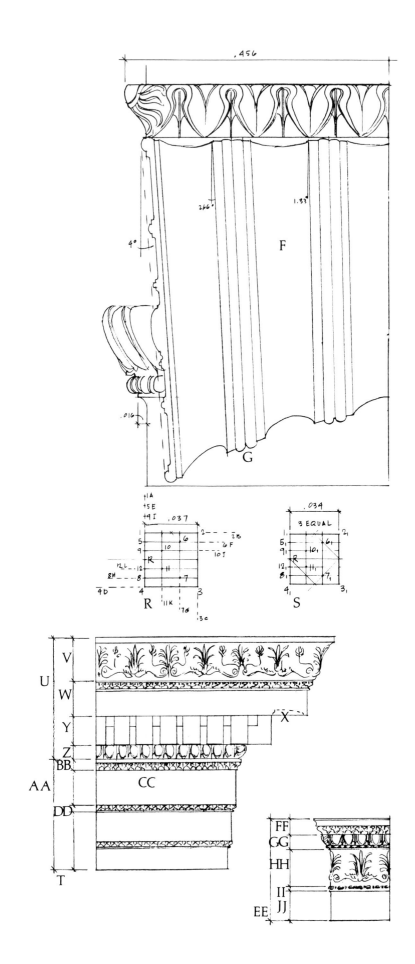

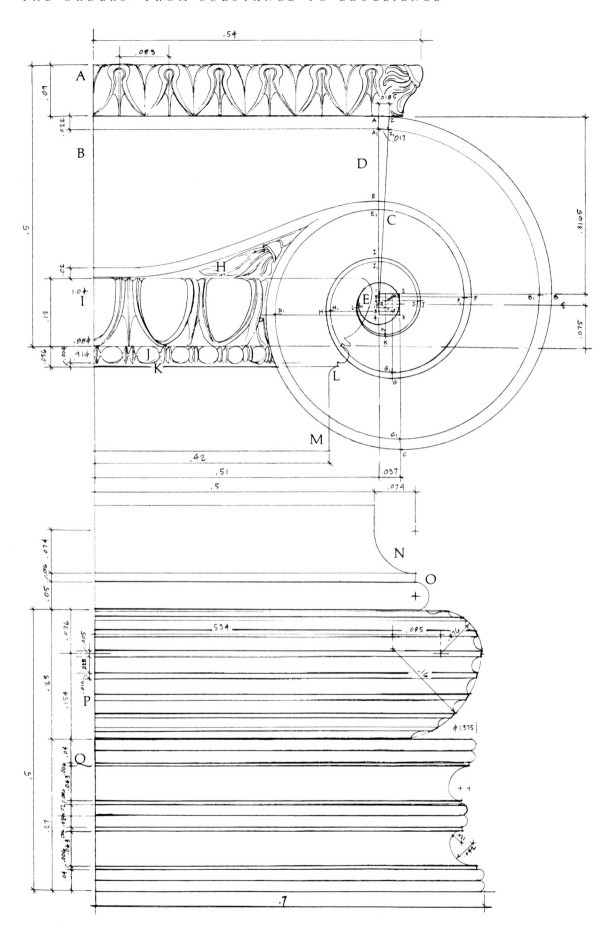

2.22. Corinthian capital, Temple of Apollo, Bassae, 430-400 B.C. (Drawn from Bauer's *Korinthische Kapitelle*.)

THE CORINTHIAN ORDER: THE PERSONIFICATION OF GRACE

The Corinthian is delicate and elaborate, traditionally identified with the character and appearance of a maiden. The legend of its genesis is presented in chapter 3. The first known architectural use of this column is in the cella of the Temple of Apollo at Bassae (fig. 2.22). A plain bell at the core is capped by an abacus with four concave sides that meet in sharp points. The bell is adorned with a series of vegetal elements. Two rows of acanthus leaves spring from the neck. Tendrils and bunchy leaves support the projecting horns of the abacus. This example displays all of the qualities that would be developed over the following 100 years to achieve a canonical form.[13]

The Corinthian column presented here is based on the first "perfect" example, the interior order of the Tholos at Epidaurus (fig. 2.23, 3.35).[14] The bell and abacus maintain their structural function while the acanthus, the fleuron, and the tendrils are carved in a naturalistic style.

Historical examples of the Corinthian entablature are less consistent than the Doric or Ionic examples. Vitruvius did not designate a specific trabeation but suggested employing an Ionic or, oddly, Doric entablature.[15] A relatively standard form was established in Roman and Renaissance practice.[16] The openness to variation that this implies ranges from subtle changes, like altering the leaves of the capital from acanthus to olive, to the radical variations seen in chapter 3.

At times architects have employed the

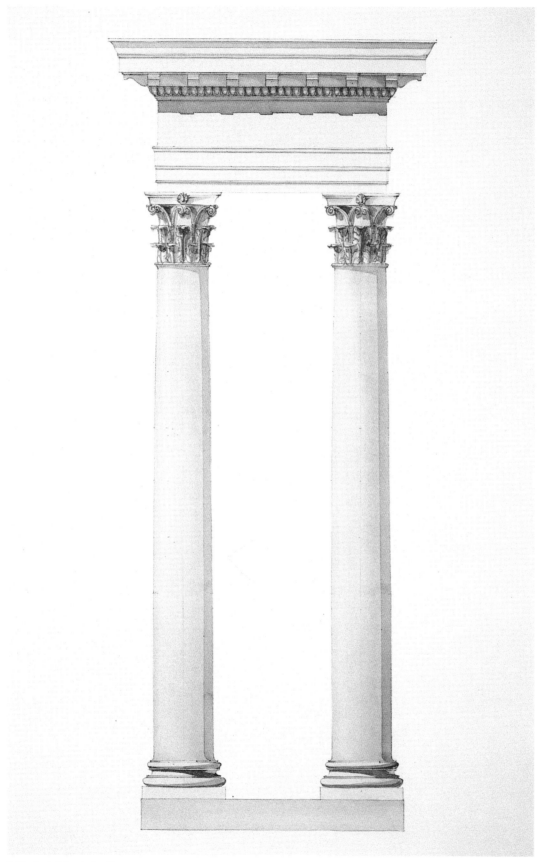

2.23. Corinthian trabeation.

2.24. Corinthian
Vocabulary
A. Entablature
B. Cornice
  C. Cyma recta Sima
  D. Corona
  E. Modillions with
cyma reversa cap
  F. Bed mold
  G. Ovolo carved
with egg and tongue
  H. Cyma reversa
carved with Lesbian leaf
mold, bead and reel
I. Frieze
  J. Apophyge (exterior
only)
K. Architrave
  L. Cyma reversa cap
molding
  M. Bead and reel
  N. Fascia
O. Column
  P. Capital
  Q. Abacus—torus,
fillet and cavetto
    R. Chamfered horn
    S. Fleuron
  T. Bell with lip
  U. Acanthus leaf
cluster
  V. Helix
  W. Spiral
  X. Cauliculus
  Y. Shaft
  Z. Astragal
  AA. Apophyge
  BB. Flute
  CC. Fillet
  DD. Apophyge
  EE. Fillet
FF. Attic base
  GG. Torus
  HH. Scotia
  II. Torus
  JJ. Plinth
KK. Fornix motif
  LL. Voussoir
  MM. Impost
  NN. Archivolt
  OO. Alette
  PP. Console

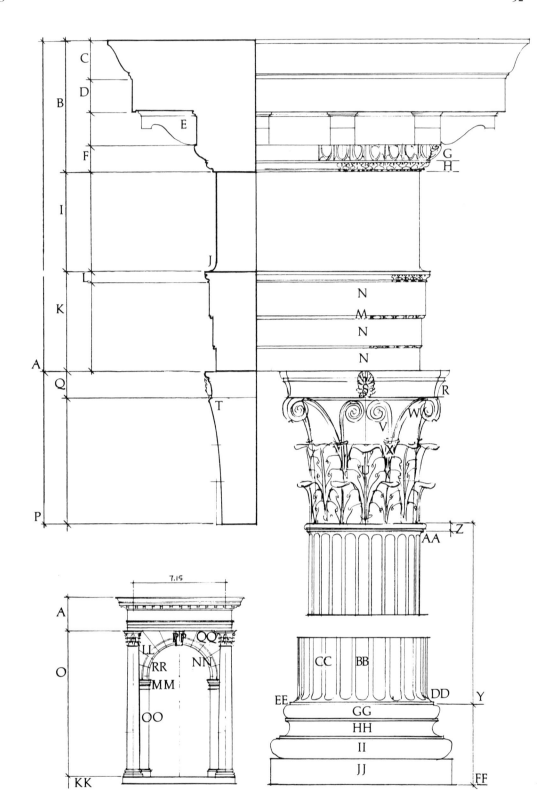

Corinthian as the exclusive order and have lost a sense of its expressive qualities through overuse. Today it needs to be used more often to counter the overreliance on Tuscan and Doric orders (fig. 2.28). None of the other orders can express the quality of grace as eloquently as the Corinthian. This quality must be readmitted to architectural vocabulary through its use (figs. 2.24-2.25).

2.25. Corinthian dimensions. The elements of the Corinthian order are depicted at four scales to show the method of construction detail.

THE COMPOSITE ORDER: THE PRONOUNCEMENT OF EBULLIENCE

The Composite is a Roman order, and with the Tuscan it enframes the three Greek orders.[17] The capital is frequently mistaken for Corinthian, but a close look reveals many formal and conceptual differences. The name of the order suggests that its elements are joined from the Ionic and Corinthian to form an amalgam.

A bell covered with clustered olive leaves supports an Ionic echinus. An abacus, similar to the Corinthian but with a rectangular fleuron, is the uppermost component (fig. 2.26). Volutes emerge from the echinus and the horns of the abacus plow through them. The volutes droop over to rest on the second tier of leaves.

Following Bernini's lead, the Composite capital should be combined with the tortuous form of the Solomonic column shaft (fig. 2.27, 2.28).[18] In this form the Composite order will have limited use, but this makes it wholly independent in its potential for expression (figs. 2.29, 2.30).

2.26. Gian Lorenzo Bernini, Baldacchino, San Pietro, Vatican, 1624-33. The baldacchino seen from the loggia of St. Veronica.

2.27. Gian Lorenzo Bernini, Baldacchino. Detail of Composite capital.

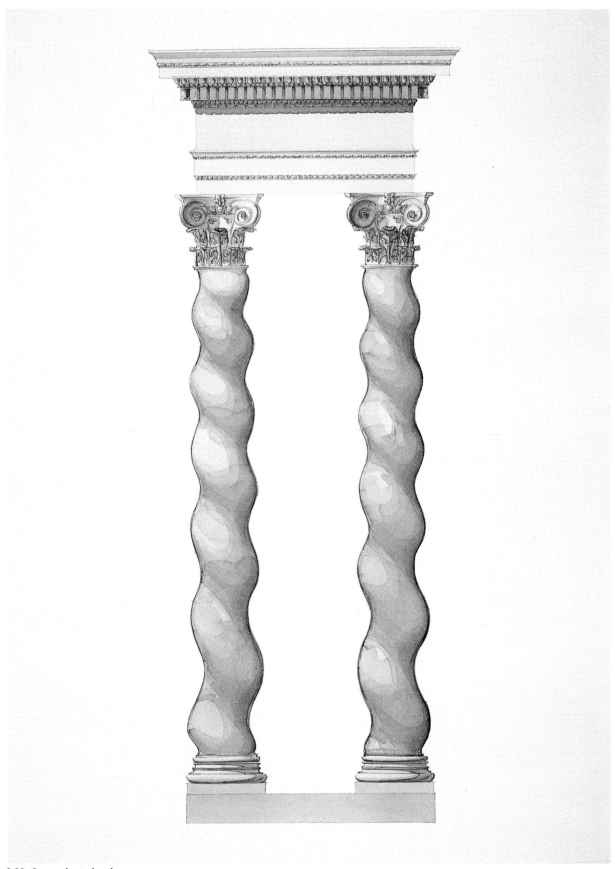

2.28. Composite trabeation

2.29. Composite
Vocabulary
A. Entablature
  B. Cornice
    C. Cyma reversa
with anthemion motif of
lotus and palmette and
bead and reel
    D. Corona with
vertical fluting
    E. Ovolo carved with
egg and tongue
    F. Dentils with pine
cone finials
    G. Bed mold, cyma
reversa carved with
Lesbian leaf and bead
and reel
  H. Frieze
    I. Apophyge
(exterior only)
    J. Architrave
    K. Cavetto and bead
and reel cap molding
    L. Cyma reversa
with carved Lesbian leaf
    M. Fascia
N. Column
  O. Capital
    P. Abacus with
chamfered horns (torus,
fillet, cavetto)
    Q. Fleuron
    R. Echinus carved
with egg and tongue
    S. Bell with fillet
and bead and reel
    T. Diagonal volutes
    U. Olive leaf clusters
    V. Bud
W. Solomonic shaft
    X. Astragal
    Y. Apophyge
    Z. Laurel leaf
festoons
    AA. Cincture
    BB. Acanthus leaves
    CC. Serpentine flutes
    DD. Apophyge
EE. "Corinthian" base
FF. Torus carved with
fasces pattern
GG. Double scotia
divided by fillets and
double roundel
HH. Torus carved with
laurel leaves
II. Plinth
JJ. Pedestal
KK. Cornice
LL. Die
MM. Base

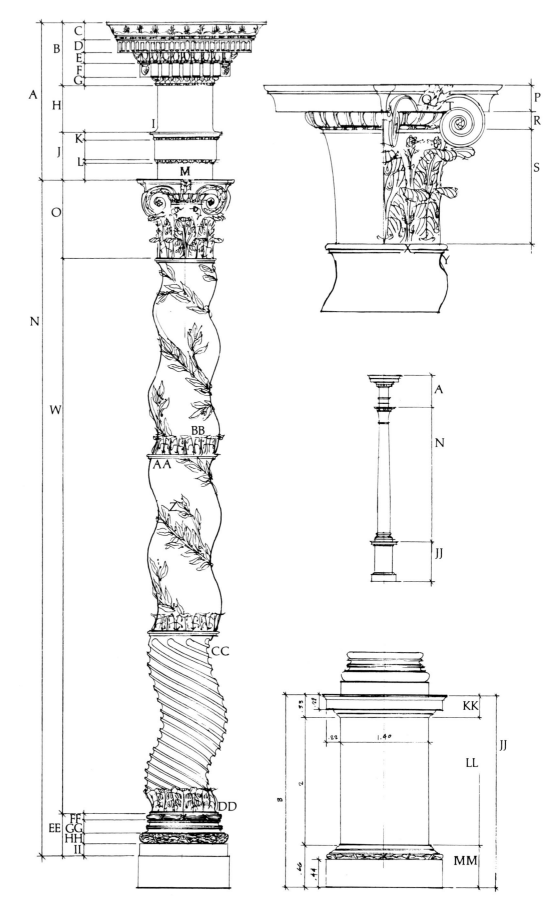

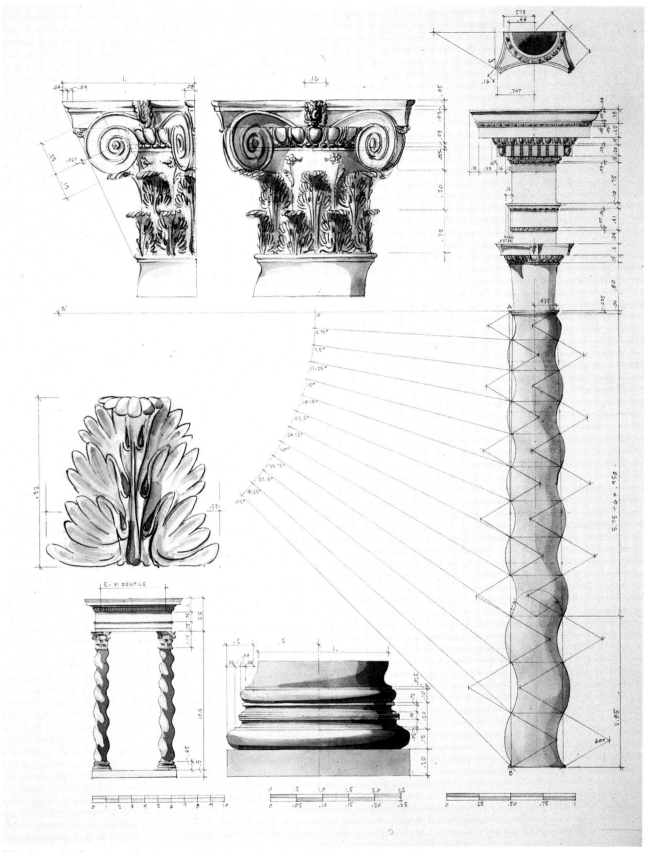

2.30. Composite dimensions. The elements of the Composite order and Solomonic shaft are depicted to show the method of construction of detail.

RULE AND INVENTION

I would not have given myself to this profession to be a mere copyist . . . I ask you to remember when I am sometimes a long way from the common designs what Michelangelo, Prince of Architects, said, "He who follows others, never goes onward."

FRANCESCO
BORROMINI [1]

VERYONE HAS A PRECONCEPTION THAT CLASSICAL architecture is regulated. Many are surprised to recognize the amount of invention required for its practice, however. Even prescribed buildings, such as Philo's Naval Arsenal (fig. 1.29), are the products of both canonical rule and invention. This chapter investigates how these concepts are distinct and how they interrelate.

RULE

He who creates the greatest disorder in architecture or in painting wants to be adored, and as if to divert himself with his disruptive inventions, and having got in his head the idea of being an architect, he has ruined as many orders and proportions as are found in the excellent and ancient works, and makes poor Vitruvius' head spin.

PIRRO LIGORIO [2]

All classical buildings are ordered, and order depends upon rule. The narrow definition of rule limits it to the value of a dictionary. Abstract, inviolable rules establish canonical orders and types of buildings. These rules objectively indicate a single way of drawing a column, for example, and are authoritarian standards. Like the dictionary, they define it, provide spelling, and offer limited advice for its usage. This notion of rule isolates the column from practical application and gives little information about fitting it into the context of a building or using it poetically.

The most basic rule is that columns are grouped into orders. The first images that the term *classical architecture* brings to mind are its signals: Tuscan, Doric, Ionic, Corinthian, and Composite columns and their entablatures—the essentials of the orders. The simplest building type of the classical system might be two Doric columns and an entablature (fig. 2.7). Two posts might support a

3.1. Invention of the Corinthian capital by Kallimachos. Watercolor by Thomas Gordon Smith.

3.2. Public washhouse near Vézeley, France, date unknown.

tems of articulation.

Some people believe that a strict concept of classicism should be maintained, and they confine it to a small range of building types. Others equate classicism exclusively with the disengaged temperament of the neoclassical period. These severe approaches define one pole of the classical tradition, but they exclude many architects who considered themselves classicists. The rigid William Chambers described Borromini as "universally and justly esteemed the most licentious and extravagant of all the modern Italians."[5] Although exponents of divergent attitudes, Chambers and Borromini share a place within the spectrum of classical architecture if we keep the definition inclusive.

PARADIGM

According to John Ruskin, classicism is " . . . an architecture invented . . . to make plagiarists of its architects, . . . in which intellect is idle, invention impossible. . . ."[6]

By calling them plagiarists, Ruskin negates the value of a fundamental method of classical architects. They imitate—both during the first steps and in accomplished practice. From designing the detail of a capital to designing a city, the architect bases and compares the work to historical models.

The Greek word *paradigma* means to show side by side. At Epidaurus the architect of the Tholos, Polykleitos the Younger, had a model Corinthian capital carved at the building site to provide a standard for those in construction (fig 3.35).[7] Since that time architects have isolated historical examples as models, as we saw in Michelangelo's drawing of the Doric order (fig. 1.23). On a larger scale, a building type can serve as the model for a new structure.

beam to form a trabeated structure, or three walls might support a gabled roof, but neither is classical unless columns and an entablature are employed.[3] One would expect a public washhouse to be a vernacular structure, but an example near Vézelay is classical because two antae and a central Tuscan column support the simple entablature and hipped roof (fig. 3.2).

The potential for elaboration on this simple theme is illustrated by the Colosseum and the Septizonium in Rome (figs. 3.3, 3.4).[4] In these buildings the orders were stacked one above the other to articulate huge volumes in one of many possible sys-

Vitruvius's hexastyle Ionic temple was Palladio's paradigm for the Villa Foscari (figs. 1.25, 1.26). More broadly, the tenor of a Golden Age can be invoked to revive an overall concept, as Palladio did by idealizing imperial Roman culture.[8]

Despite attempts to define standards, none are immutable. Models are established that initiate only a fleeting synthesis. Once the paradigm is applied to the problem at hand, its form must be altered to accommodate the constraints of reality. As one becomes increasingly literate, more rigor is required to choose standards because one has more choices from which to select. Paradigms impose limitations as well as provide inspiration. We are never liberated from them because they are not only resources; they become the standard against which new work is evaluated.

For some, Vitruvius's name conjures visions of overdependence on rule; they fear that this force inhibits creativity and spontaneity. Conversely, others depend on the false hope that a canon contains formulae which, once plugged in, automatically solve challenging architectural problems. Vitruvius invites this expectation when he writes that the architect " . . . may find the proportions stated by which he can construct correct and faultless examples of temples in the Doric fashion."[9] His description of the tetrastyle Doric temple defines the building to a remarkable degree by providing the height, diameter, and dimensions of the columns, the form of its capital, and the composition of its entablature (fig. 3.5). The minute detail and qualitative aspects of the design are unclear, however, because Vitruvius naturally made assumptions of architectural knowledge common to his time, and he could not convey subjective aspects through words alone.

3.3. Colosseum, Rome, A.D. 80. Superposed Doric and Ionic orders in the fornix motif.

3.4. Septizonium of Septimius Severus, Rome, A.D. 203. Destroyed by Sixtus V in the late 1500s. From a drawing by Jan Bruegel showing the gate to San Gregorio Magno on the right and the Arch of Constantine in the distance. (Fototeca Unione, at the American Academy in Rome, F.U. 6627F).

3.5. Tetrastyle, prostyle Doric temple according to Vitruvius, first century B.C., ***Ten Books,*** **bk. IV, chs. III-V. Wash by Thomas Gordon Smith.**

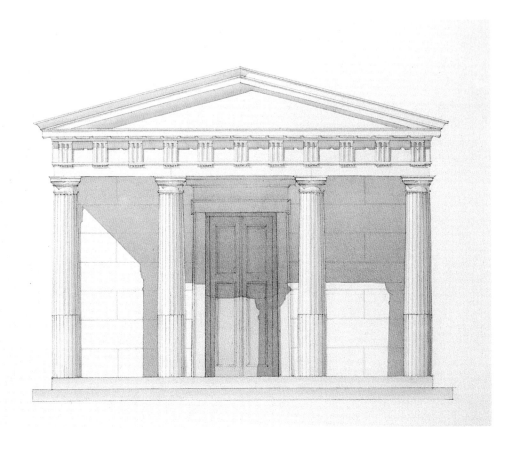

We may sometimes fear that rule will overwhelm our independence, but this does not take its real function into account. Rule exists to maintain the basic form, meaning, and character of the order, and it has accomplished this with remarkable continuity. If we compare Vitruvius's version of the Doric temple to structures built before and after his time, we see that his standard for proportion and detail is not universal, but it does codify a consistent type.

Vitruvius based his formulae on the Hellenistic temples of Asia Minor, and his Doric is similar in detail to the Temple of Hera Basilea at Pergamon (fig. 3.6).[10] The continuity of rule seen here is demonstrated even more effectively when we see Vitruvius as the inspiration for Palladio's

application of the Doric tetrastyle at the Villa Pisani at Montagnana (fig. 3.7).[11] This engaged frontispiece is drawn here as a freestanding element to emphasize that when rule predominates and an architect understands the language, the written word can convey very specific lessons over time. Through the interpretations of Bramante, Palladio, and others, Vitruvius conveyed the ideals of the Hellenistic age to modern times, and these forms provide a gauge against which we intuitively judge buildings from other times and places.

Many Doric buildings possess the same components as Vitruvius's temple but stem from a different time or aesthetic and demonstrate the variety that exists even within rule. The provincial sixth-century B.C. temple at Foce del Sele demonstrates

3.6. (Top left) Temple of
Hera Basileia,
Pergamon, 159-138 B.C.
Wash by Thomas
Gordon Smith. (Drawn
from Schazmann,
*Altertümer von
Pergamon.*)

3.7. (Top right) Andrea
Palladio, engaged Doric
tetrastyle, Villa Pisani,
Montagnana, 1555.
(Drawn from Bertotti
Scamozzi, *Le Fabbriche.*)

3.8. (Center left) Doric
temple, Foce del Sele,
near Paestum, sixth
century B.C. (Drawn from
Zancani, *Heraion.*)

3.9. (Center right)
Treasury of the
Athenians, Delphi,
490 B.C. (Drawn from
Hoff, *Fouilles de
Delphes.*)

3.10. (Bottom left)
Temple of Apollo of the
Athenians, Delos,
425 B.C. (Drawn from
Courby, *Délos.*)

3.11. (Bottom right)
Temple of Hercules,
Cori, c. 75 B.C. (Drawn
from Delbrueck,
Hellenistische Bauten.)

the bulging forms of the archaic Doric order as it developed in Italy (fig. 3.8).[12] The Treasury of the Athenians at Delphi is more refined than Foce del Sele, but its proportions are heavy when compared to its Vitruvian successors (fig. 3.9).[13] Although more refined than Delphi, the Temple of the Athenians at Delos is akin to the most popular ideal of Doric perfection—the Parthenon; yet it still seems robust when compared to the wide column spacing and brittle moldings of the Hellenistic/Vitruvian standard (fig. 3.10).[14]

A final ancient example, the Temple of Hercules at Cori, demonstrates a bizarre alternative to Vitruvius's system of proportion (fig. 3.11).[15] Its slender columns and thin moldings depart from the Doric and are more in tune with the character of a Hellenistic Ionic temple. It is so different from the other examples that we might wonder if Cori deserves Doric status at all.

During the baroque period architects employed the Corinthian and Composite orders to fulfill their desire for exuberant forms. Francesco Borromini stood alone in his perception of the Doric. In his sober Palazzo Banco Santo Spirito, Borromini varied the Vitruvian proportions by elongating the pilasters and creating uneven metopes. Despite these transgressions against rule, the structure maintains the character of the Doric order (fig. 3.12).[16]

Borromini made the window aediculae at the Palazzo della Propaganda Fide into a display of the Doric that is both florid and archaeological (figs. 1.24, 3.13).[17] He borrowed an unusual triglyph from an ancient example, and the column shafts

3.12. Francesco Borromini, Palazzo Spada/Banco Santo Spirito, Rome, 1661. Wash by Thomas Gordon Smith. (Drawn from Borromini. Elevations published in Heimburger–Rivalli, "Disegni Sconosciuti.")

3.13. Francesco Borromini, Doric window aedicula, Palazzo della Propaganda Fide, Rome, 1654-62. Wash by Thomas Gordon Smith. (Drawn from photos in Portoghesi, *Borromini*.)

have no bases. Borromini must have been proud of gleaning this authentic Greek feature from Vitruvius and the Theater of Marcellus.[18] The aedicula is different in proportion from Vitruvius's temple, but a comparison reveals numerous instances of rule woven with invention.

Borromini's baroque interpretation of the rigid Doric in a curved format is an example of what provoked some eighteenth-century architects, like Chambers, to call him licentious. Others admired his ability to express the Doric in dynamic forms.

The Bohemian Kilian Ignaz Dientzenhofer developed the side portal of Sv. Tomaš in Prague as a concave Doric aedicula (fig. 3.14).[19] The columns and pilasters are clumped at the corners of the entablature and, like Borromini's prototype, it supports an exuberant pediment. Borromini and Dientzenhofer produced dynamic buildings that took the Doric to its limits without contradicting its character. Dientzenhofer maintains credibility, despite the jumble of elements in his capitals and the cubistic entablature, by rendering the triglyphs and molding in a precise, academic way (fig. 3.15).

By utilizing Vitruvius's temple as a reference point, we see that rule maintains formal consistency even if the proportions are altered and the methods of organizing the elements are modified. The four Greek examples at Foce del Sele, Delphi, Delos, and Pergamon show a development toward the refinement of proportion and detail. The elegant Hellenistic type at Pergamon was the paradigm for Vitruvius, and his authority convinced Palladio to perpetuate the form although he had no firsthand knowledge of Greek buildings.

Apart from the proportional and poetic adjustments we have surveyed, radical

3.14. Kilian Ignaz Dientzenhofer, Doric aedicula of side portal, Sv. Tomaš, Prague, 1724-31.

3.15. Kilian Ignaz Dientzenhofer, detail of capitals and cubistic Doric entablature, Sv. Tomaš.

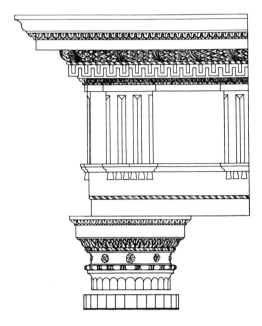

3.16. Baths of Diocletian, Doric capital and entablature, Rome, A.D. 300. (From *Cyclopedia of Architecture*.)

3.17. Gilles-Marie Oppenort, proposal for a Doric entablature, c. 1695. (Courtesy of Cooper-Hewitt Museum, The Smithsonian Institution's National Museum of Design; purchased in memory of Sarah, Eleanor and Amy Hewitt, 1960-102-26 recto, detail.)

changes in the Doric generally indicate misunderstanding instead of invention. A Doric capital and entablature from the Baths of Diocletian is decadent because acanthus leaves cover the echinus, and dentils, a distinctly Ionic feature, support the cornice (fig. 3.16).[20] A decorative handling of all elements contradicts the character of the Doric, as well.

A sketch from the notebooks of the French architect Gilles-Marie Oppenort denies the architectonic qualities of the Doric in a similar manner (fig. 3.17).[21] During his stay in Rome in the 1690s, Oppenort was devoted to the accurate documentation of Borromini's buildings. His own design for an entablature lacks understanding of Borromini's rationale, however. The elements are rendered as superficial motifs rather than as forms that signify structural function. Feathery brackets replace the triglyphs, and the mutules are recessed into the soffit. Worst of all, the guttae are rendered as shallow depressions in the architrave, not as pegs.

Because the Doric is unsuited for elaboration it should not be adorned in these ways. On the other hand, there are successful examples which convey Doric character by abstracting its elements. The architect of the peristyle at the Villa della Torre near Verona suggested the rude origins of the order by replacing the columns with piers of randomly-sized rusticated stones (fig. 3.18).[22] These support an architrave capped by a giant cavetto. Though the triglyphs and metopes are deleted, a taenia divides the two zones and reveals the architect's intention to mark out the rhythm of the frieze with evenly spaced regulae and guttae.

Today we accept diversity with an attitude that is overly pluralistic and shy away from one function of rule—to strive toward

3.18. Villa della Torre, two rusticated piers and the Doric entablature of the peristyle, Fumane, near Verona, c. 1530.

3.19. Pietro da Cortona, Dinocrates displays his vision of a city for Mt. Athos to Alexander the Great, c. 1660. Cortona depicts himself presenting an architectural proposal to Pope Alexander VII in a clever interpretation of the Vitruvian legend. The now clothed Dinocrates is shown sponsoring Cortona, referring to impressive antique precedent. Drawing on paper. (Reproduced by courtesy of the Trustees of the British Museum.)

a universal. Though it loosens in practice, the rigor of rule is necessary because the canon aids learning and helps to maintain the authenticity of classical forms. The development of a Doric canon requires the reappraisal of its essential elements. As I did in chapter 2, one must look back to origins to decide which details are appropriate to the character of the order. Despite its positive value, however, the canon cannot be sacrosanct. Respect for rule is appropriate; reverence is not.

INVENTION

Classical architecture has been developed by architects of varying temperaments. They range in type from the strict and didactic Hermogenes, credited with having codified the Ionic order,[23] to the impulsive Dinocrates, who had visions of building a city sculpted from Mt. Athos for Alexander the Great (fig. 3.19).[24] From the epigrams

that begin this chapter, we see that the same extremes of mentality existed during the Renaissance and baroque periods. This reflects a natural spectrum of personality, but also indicates the opposing impulses that we strive to resolve in life. Despite his diatribes against the mannerists, Ligorio was architect of the imaginative fountains at the Villa d'Este. No matter how fantastic, Borromini's designs indicate a rigor that came partly from his apprenticeship under

3.20. Gian Lorenzo Bernini, tetrastyle temple front of the portico of Piazza San Pietro, Vatican, 1657-67.

the dour Maderno. Although Borromini distinguished himself from the "copyists" around him, he emulated Michelangelo's motifs through life. We like to think in extremes, and Ligorio and Borromini might personify rule and invention for us, but in reality neither was all rational nor all intuitive.

If rule derives from the impulse to reduce classical architecture to its essence, the opposite tendency—invention—opens to manifoldness. Invention is a product of improvisation influenced by the standards of a model solution.

Many problems require invention. The impetus may be to solve a utilitarian difficulty. It can be an accommodation for perceptual distortions. But most importantly, invention is used to achieve rhetorical effect. To be effective, expression must incorporate three interrelated principles—character, iconography, and spectrum.

CHARACTER OF THE ORDERS

The principle of character seems to have developed during the Hellenistic period. Prior to that the majority of temples in Western Greece were Doric, whether dedicated to Zeus, Apollo, Athena, Poseidon, or Hera. The comparative refinement of these buildings was a product of chronology, not the expression of each god's attributes.[25]

With the combination of the Ionic and Corinthian orders within a Doric structure, the distinctions between the orders led to a physical analogy between the column and a human being (fig. 2.1).[26] Vitruvius subscribed to this belief and linked each order to aspects of gender, age, and personality in a crude but understandable formula. He used this analogy to determine the appropriate order to represent the deity of a temple. In the Renaissance Serlio adapted the notion to Christian subjects.[27] Thus, the Doric order is appropriate to forceful males like Hercules and St. Peter. The Ionic conveys

3.21. Gian Lorenzo Bernini, tetrastyle aedicula at the Capella Cornaro, Santa Maria della Vittoria, Rome, 1644-47.

3.22. Temple of Hercules, Cori, c. 75 B.C. (Fototeca Unione, at the American Academy in Rome, F.U. 19769.)

the character of Bacchus or Hera. The Corinthian order is compared to a young girl through its slender, fastidious form.

The Tuscan and Composite orders were not included in this analogy, but Renaissance and baroque architects deemed the Tuscan appropriate to the expression of rudimentary character and reserved the Composite for functions more elevated than the Corinthian, as in Bernini's Baldacchino at St. Peter's (fig. 2.27).[28]

Personifying Doric, Ionic, and Corinthian in anthropomorphic categories is an expedient to gaining a more subtle understanding of their role in expressing the function of a building. In practice, this character becomes more intimately understood and spreads to other components. Portals, window surrounds, architectural ornament, painted decoration, and the selection of material should relate to the character of the particular order.

In the Tuscan/Doric portico of the Piazza

at St. Peter's, Bernini chose travertine to reinforce the sturdiness of the architecture (fig. 3.20). By contrast, he executed the Corinthian aedicula that shelters his statue of St. Teresa in Ecstasy in marble and gilt bronze (fig. 3.21).[29]

When an architect neglects the connection between material and the correct proportions of an order, the result can be an ugly hybrid such as the Temple of Hercules at Cori (fig. 3.22).

The task of determining a suitable order for a building is probably the least tangible aspect of working with the classical system. One begins by considering the function of a building and what ideas it should embody. This may be quite simple: Tuscan for a washhouse. Complex buildings require more consideration of which order to use, or in many cases, which combination of orders to use; yet the architect must strive to be comprehensible in communicating the ideas of the building.

3.23. Francesco Borromini, portal from the balcony to the library at the Oratorio dei Filippini, Rome, 1638. The portal is a variation on Michelangelo's design for the Laurentian Library in Florence.

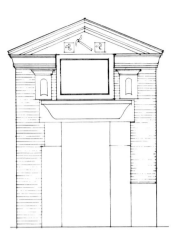
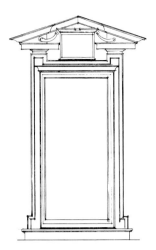

3.24-3.26. Comparison of portal designs by Michelangelo and Borromini to a mausoleum facade now in the catacombs of San Sebastiano in Rome (3.24). Michelangelo's portal at the Ricetto of the Laurentian Library in Florence of c. 1533 (3.25) and Borromini's variation on the theme for the Cappelletta di San Filippo Neri of 1638 (3.26) at the Oratorio dei Filippini in Rome, may derive from this ancient form in which an inscription tablet breaks into the pediment. Drawing by Thomas Gordon Smith.

3.27. Antonio Raggi, San Carlo Borromeo, travertine sculpture in the central niche of Borromini's San Carlo alle Quattro Fontane, Rome, after 1667.

ICONOGRAPHY AND LITERAL EXPRESSION

If character conveys a general concept, iconography offers the potential for buildings to communicate literal ideas. The orders are relatively mute, but sculpted and painted figures articulate ideas more fully. The storytelling sculpture of Greece and the elaborate painting schemes of the Italian baroque are models for this. It is time to reincorporate these arts with architecture.

An iconographic program can also operate on a less tangible plane by alluding to literary and cultural associations. Connors calls Borromini's development of material and ornament in the Oratorio dei Filippini facade "didactic communication" and ascribes meaning to the architect's selection of various types of brick in relation to their uses in specific ancient and Renaissance structures (figs. 1.16, 1.34).[30]

Borromini designed a portal at the center of the facade that makes more obvious references (fig. 3.23). The dove of the Holy Spirit hovers above the doorway. The emblems of San Filippo Neri, the lily and the eight-pointed star, are visible on the door frame. The architect devised a literal anthropomorphism by swelling the casings into the form of ears, an appropriate symbol for a building that functions for the praise of the "God who hears."

Inside the oratory a similar door to the reliquary chapel of St. Filippo Neri (fig. 3.26) is based on a Michelangelo portal at the Laurentian Library (fig. 3.25). I suspect that Borromini was doing more, however, than making a variation on this Renaissance theme. Both designs bear a striking resemblance to a common type of ancient mausoleum (fig. 3.24), and it is possible that Borromini used this symbol of death to commemorate the Christian saint.

To transmit certain ideas the architect must employ the human figure. Antonio Raggi's poignant travertine sculpture of Carlo Borromeo stands in the central niche of Borromini's church at the Quattro Fontane (fig. 3.27). It conveys the transporting energy that made the saint a paradigm for the baroque spirit.[31]

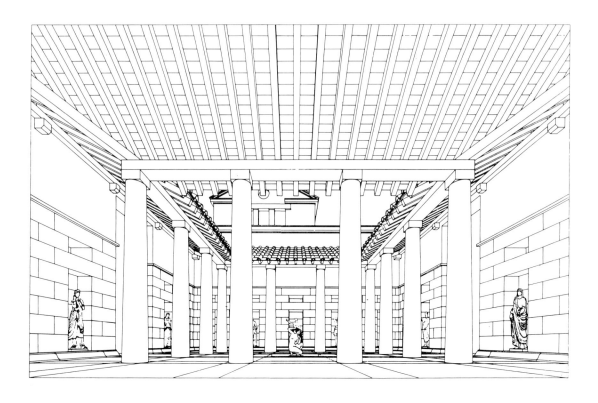

3.28. Manuel Iñiguez and Alberto Ustarroz, a peri-style court in their reconstruction of Pliny's Lauren-tian Villa, 1981. (From Culot, *La Laurentine*.)

SPECTRUM:
RANGE OF EXPRESSION

All five orders—Tuscan, Doric, Ionic, Corinthian, and Composite—must be used to express a range of character. When practice gravitates to a single order the capacity to be expressive is limited. The richness of the Corinthian order and the overpowering quality of the Composite may reflect the aspirations of Imperial Rome, but the almost exclusive use of these orders by the Romans contradicts the differentiation of character advocated by Vitruvius. By contrast, during the seventeenth century Northern Europeans were overly dependent on the Tuscan order.[32]

Focusing on one order ignores the possibilities for communication that come with using the entire spectrum. This erodes the essence of the order and it becomes multipurpose. In today's practice there is a tendency to overuse the Tuscan; in fact, it is often abstracted by designing untapered

3.31. Johann Michael Fischer, Santa Maria Zwiefalten, 1741-65. Sketch of Corinthian capital by Thomas Gordon Smith.

3.29. Donato Bramante, spiral ramp, Vatican Belvedere, before 1512.

3.30. Carlo Maderno, Santa Susanna, Rome, 1603. Detail of Corinthian capital and entablature at transition from the travertine to the brick facade.

columns without capitals. The rationalistic projects of Manuel Iñiguez and Alberto Ustarroz are among the better examples (fig. 3.28).[33] As the most rudimentary order, Tuscan is most easily integrated with the modernist's preference for abstraction. When the Tuscan becomes the only order utilized it fails to signify its own character, because it is not seen in contrast with the more refined connotations of Ionic or Corinthian. All orders must be kept on the palette.

Not every building needs to use the full spectrum of orders, but Bramante used all five in the spiral ramp at the Vatican Belvedere with interesting results (fig. 3.29). Tuscan and Doric begin the lower turns, progress through Ionic, and mount to Corinthian and Composite at the top. All the columns bear the same entablature to emphasize the basic unity of the orders.

A spectrum of expression is also possible within an order, moving either toward reduction or elaboration. From the canonical form, a series of graduated simplifications concludes with the abstract pilaster strip. At Santa Susanna, Maderno used brick pilaster strips in contrast to the developed Corinthian piers and engaged columns of the travertine facade (figs. 1.14, 1.15, 3.30). The profile of the entablature is reduced in projection and this simplification reinforces the idea of spectrum. Rococo variations on the Corinthian capital generally move toward greater elaboration. These go to the limits of enthusiasm in Bavarian baroque churches (fig. 3.31)

A wide variety of expression is possible within the canonical spectrum of Tuscan, Doric, Ionic, Corinthian, and Composite. Spectrum provides the theoretical basis for articulating the orders in buildings. Without it, the classical language is babble—simply a collection of miscellaneous elements without organization or the capacity for expression. If the spectrum of the orders is approached with openness, the invention of "new" orders is superfluous.

3.32. The invention of the Corinthian capital by Kallimachos. Preparatory sketch for watercolor by Thomas Gordon Smith.

THE CORINTHIAN CAPITAL: AN ANALOGUE FOR INVENTION

The third order . . . called Corinthian, imitates the slight figure of a maiden; because girls are represented with slighter dimensions because of their tender age, and admit of more graceful effects in ornament. Now the first invention of that capital is related to have happened thus. A girl, a native of Corinth, already of age to be married, was attacked by disease and died. After her funeral, the goblets which delighted her when living, were put together in a basket by her nurse, carried to the monument, and placed on the top. That they might remain longer, exposed as they were to the weather, she covered the basket with a tile. As it happened the basket was placed upon the root of an acanthus. Meanwhile about spring time, the root of the acanthus, being pressed down in the middle by the weight, put forth leaves and shoots. The shoots grew up the sides of the basket and, being pressed down at the angles by the force of the weight of the tile, were compelled to form the curves of

volutes at the extreme parts. Then Kallimachus, who for the elegance and refinement of his marble carving was nicknamed Katatechnos by the Athenians, passing the monument, perceived the basket and the young leaves growing up. Pleased with the style and novelty of the grouping, he made columns for the Corinthians on this model and fixed the proportions.

VITRUVIUS IV, I [54]

The inspiration that led Kallimachos to fabricate the prototypical Corinthian capital associates the order with spontaneity (figs. 3.1, 3.32).[35] How many people had come to the maiden's grave to grieve, or had passed it on their way to Corinth, without noting this poignant token of devotion? It took an eye on the lookout for solutions to sculptural problems to perceive an architectural form in the basket, tile, and acanthus. All stories of genesis are idealized, but those who invent things can identify with this account. We have all experienced flashes of recognition in response to a sudden perception of ordinary objects. According to Vitruvius's tale, the Corinthian capital had its genesis in a natural accident!

The first known Corinthian capital was used in the Temple of Apollo at Bassae (fig. 3.33).[36] Fifty years later the sculptor Skopas further developed this type at Tegea, a squat capital with bunchy leaves (fig. 3.34).[37] Though Vitruvius states that Kallimachos "fixed" the Corinthian proportions, it took 100 years of sculptural refinement before Polykleitos the Younger formulated the elegant standard we recognize today at the Tholos at Epidaurus (fig. 3.35).

The capitals of the Pantheon in Rome are similar to the Epidaurus type (fig. 3.37). The structural features, the bell and the abacus, are solid, while the ornament is intentionally superficial. Two tiers of leaves spring above the astragal. On each face, one set of

(Upper left to lower right)

3.33. Iktinos, Corinthian capital, Temple of Apollo, Bassae, 430-400 B.C. The washes that illustrate 3.33-3.35 are drawn after Bauer's *Korinthische Kapitelle.*)

3.34. Skopas, Corinthian capital, Temple of Athena Alea, Tegea, 370-340 B.C.

3.35. Polykleitos the Younger, Corinthian capital, Tholos, Epidaurus, 360-330 B.C.

3.36. Antiochus Epiphanes, Corinthian capital, Bouleterion, Miletus, 175-164 B.C. (Drawn from Robertson, *Greek and Roman Architecture.*)

3.37. Corinthian capitals of a column and pier of the portico, Pantheon, Rome, A.D. 125. (Fototeca Unione at the American Academy in Rome, F.U. 14444.)

3.38. *Acanthus Mollis* in spring with bud of flower beginning to form.

tendrils supports the horns of the abacus and another pair frames the fleuron. In detail the Roman type is different from the Greek paradigm. The curve of the Pantheon abacus is more extreme, and the ends of the horns are chamfered. The leaf has been changed from an acanthus to an olive, and the formerly stylized tendrils now spring from a cauliculus, an acanthus stalk.[38]

Although the Pantheon may be held up as a standard for the Corinthian capital, its form is not immutable. The rich, decorative elements provide many opportunities for variation. Beyond this, the Corinthian is inherently open to variation in a way that the Doric is not. It was invented in a cemetery, and its principal decorative element is a plant that any gardener will recognize as unstoppable (fig. 3.38). The notion of regeneration is revealed in the capitals of the propylon of the Bouleterion at Miletus. The germlike sprouts that strive upward assure renewal (fig. 3.36).[39]

The most basic reason to alter the Corinthian paradigm is formal. As we see in the portico of the Pantheon, when a freestanding column is related to a wall, its elements are transformed to correspond to the square shape of a pier or pilaster (fig. 3.37). This is beautifully accomplished at the Pantheon, but the capital of another Roman pier is adapted less successfully. Its broad sides are sculpted in accord with the canonical model, but the narrow flank is only half of this width. The architect simply squeezed the elements together to make a graceless variation (fig. 3.39).[40] The cluster of Corinthian pilaster capitals at Sant' Andrea al Quirinale demonstrates how Bernini designed harmonious capitals to solve an even more difficult geometrical problem (fig. 3.40).

Making variations on the typical Corinthian form is one aspect of invention.

3.39. Corinthian capital of a rectangular pier of unknown provenance, in the Museo Nazionale Romano, Rome, c. A.D. 10.

3.40. Gian Lorenzo Bernini, Corinthian capitals of the cluster of pilasters of the giant order, Sant' Andrea al Quirinale, Rome, 1658-72.

3.41. Guarino Guarini, Corinthian pilaster capital with instruments of the Passion, Capella della Santissima Sindone, Torino, 1668.

3.43. Negative image of the "Man of the Shroud," the relic believed to be the linen in which Christ's body was wrapped for burial, Capella della Santissima Sindone, Torino.

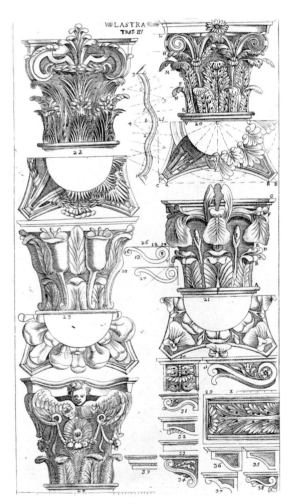

3.42. Guarino Guarini, *Architettura Civile*, plate VIII from Tratatto III, illustrates Guarini's fertile variations on the Corinthian capital. Originally published 1686, this edition 1737.

Altering its form to make rhetorical statements brings us to a deeper conceptual level. About 1668 Guarino Guarini designed a set of pilaster capitals for the Capella della Santissima Sindone in Torino (fig. 3.41). These capitals are similar to a number of florid inventions illustrated in his treatise, but Guarini modified them for the unique function of the Sindone (fig. 3.42).[41] The chapel is a gigantic reliquary for the linen shroud in which Christ is believed to have been wrapped after the descent from the cross. Tradition says that His image was imprinted upon it (fig. 3.43).[42] Guarini rendered the crisp olive leaves and sinuous tendrils of the capitals in grey-green bronze and applied objects to these standard forms to remind us of the crucifixion. He ringed the upper leaves with a crown of thorns as a symbol of Christ's humiliation. The fleuron is affixed to the abacus with three spikes and its petals reach out in anthropomorphic reaction to the puncture. The superscription *INRI* flails with turmoil. By imbuing the instruments of the Passion with animate qualities, Guarini assured that our comprehension of these symbols, already loaded with associations, is more keen.

Going beyond symbolism, figural sculpture can be combined with the elements of the capital to convey ideas. The Corinthian and the similar Composite capitals are more open to this development than either Doric or Ionic. Hundreds of figured Corinthian and Composite capitals survive from antiquity, but few are found among the simpler orders.[43] An impressive Composite capital from the Baths of Caracalla has a miniature figure of Hercules carved above the first tier of leaves (fig. 3.44). The capital now rests on the floor of the ruined baths and Hercules is seen plainly, but in its original position it was high above the floor, and this gesture to infuse the capital with qualities of strength and virility was not so apparent.

The Vitruvian association between character and order would suggest that Doric best conveys Hercules. A statue defines his temperament. A detail of the head displays sternness and physical strength and gives the impression of a man willing to execute barbarous deeds (fig. 3.45).[44] The hero wears his consistent attribute, the flayed skin of the Nemean lion, a beast he choked to free Nemea from its ravages. After it was killed, Hercules removed the lion's impenetrable pelt with its own claws.[45]

Hercules wore this spoil as his only garment, and the now flaccid leonine face forms the helmet of a cape secured across his chest by knotting the front paws. The lion skin takes many forms in sculpture—a little rumpled when draped over a tree stump in the capital from the Baths of Caracalla (an imitation of the "Farnese Hercules" composition), or reanimated when worn as a helmet. This pelt and his

3.44. Composite capital with figure of Hercules carved in high relief, Baths of Caracalla, A.D. 211-37, Rome. (Fototeca Unione at the American Academy in Rome, F.U. 3559F.)

3.45. Hercules, detail of head, Roman copy of a Greek fourth-century B.C. original. (The Metropolitan Museum of Art, gift of Mrs. Frederick F. Thompson, 1903; 03.12.14.)

3.46. Corinthian capital wrapped with the flayed pelt of the Nemean lion, from a circular shrine dedicated to Hercules, Rome, c. A.D. 50. (Vatican Museum, Galleria dei Candelabri; inv. 2479.)

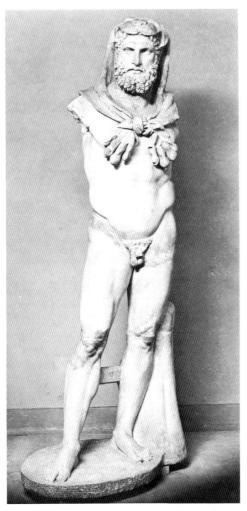

3.47. Standing Hercules. Roman copy of a Greek
fourth-century B.C. original. (The Metropolitan
Museum of Art, gift of Mrs. Frederick F. Thompson,
1903; 03.12.14.)

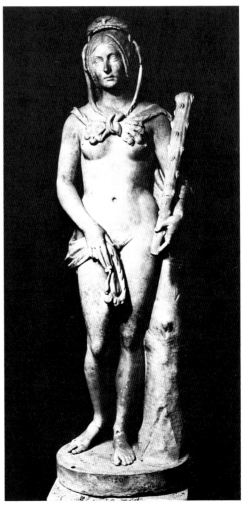

3.48. Portrait Statue in the form of Omphale, Rome,
c. A.D. 200. (Vatican Museum, Museo Gregoriano
Profano; inv. 4385.)

oaken club have been Hercules' emblems
since archaic times.

Three "Herculean" Corinthian capitals
and a section of an architrave provide a tan-
talizing glimpse of how an emblem can be
combined with the forms of a capital to
convey ideas that go beyond symbolism.
These objects, discovered in Rome in 1881,
are the only remains of a circular shrine
dedicated to Hercules during the Augustan
period (fig. 3.46).[46] The overall shape and
proportions of the capitals indicate that they

are Corinthian. The bell is tightly wrapped
with the Nemean pelt crushing the leaves,
fleuron, and tendrils of the Pantheon
model. The lion's face forms a leering grin
stretched across the front, and the folds of
the eyes are pulled back tautly. The paws
are brought up to support the horns of the
abacus, and the tail is cinched around to
bind the skin to the bell. The teeth are
ineffectually bared, but the curly mane still
crowns this beast. One shudders to imagine
the prototype of these provocative

3.49. Temple of Hercules at the Forum Boarium, Rome, c. 75 B.C. (Fototeca Unione at the American Academy in Rome, F.U. 6268.)

elements—blood dripping from the pelt and running down the column shaft.

Few images are farther from Vitruvius's maidenly Corinthian order than the contorted image of this brilliant concept. The contradiction of decorum reminds one of Omphale, the Lydian queen who purchased Hercules as a slave and exchanged her feminine garments for his Nemean cloak and club. A Roman portrait sculpture of an adventuresome matron in the guise of Omphale illustrates the contradiction inher-ent in the columns of the Hercules shrine (fig. 3.47, 3.48).[47]

Though the Romans enshrined Hercules in Corinthian structures beginning with his Temple at the Forum Boarium, this practice was conceptually wrong (fig. 3.49).[48] In the Hercules shrine, the Nemean capitals rectify this situation; the maidenly connotations of the order are cancelled and the character of the hero is reinforced by these paradoxical examples of invention (fig. 3.50).

3.50. Circular shrine dedicated to Hercules on the Tiber, Rome, c. A.D. 150. This reconstruction is based on three capitals, a section of the entablature and the excavator's drawings of the plan. The site was discovered in the late nineteenth century during construction of the Tiber River embankments. Water color by Thomas Gordon Smith.

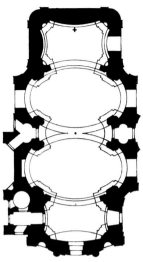

INVENTION AND THE VERNACULAR

The rationalizing tendency of rule and the accommodating capacity of invention may be separated in theory, but they are interdependent in practice. The object is to recognize the different natures of these forces and to work with them simultaneously. We balance these contradictions constantly when we discipline our daily routine in spite of the inventive spontaneity of our personalities. With invention, classical architecture gains broad limits, but some buildings fall outside its boundaries.

As the tradition of classical architecture has moved from its points of initial development in Greece and Turkey, the canons have been exposed to diverse cultures, materials, climatic conditions, and indigenous architectural traditions. In many cases, architects have learned ways to accommodate everyday requirements while maintaining a regulated classical system of ordering. Christoph Dientzenhofer's castle

church at Smiřice, north of Prague, is a classical structure despite the steep pitch of its slate roof, the onion steeple, and the application of Gothic ribbing on the vault of the guitar-shaped plan (fig. 3.51).[49] Though accommodations like this have enriched the classical tradition, they must be kept in shape by periodic realignment to remain classical. Christoph's son, Kilian Ignaz Dientzenhofer, practiced this procedure. He formalized his father's plan type from Smiřice and made his orders conform to a more academically correct standard at the church of Sv. František Xaverský in Oparany (fig. 3.52).[50]

If rule and invention are not held in tension, the practice of classical architecture becomes either anarchistic or pedantic. Pedantic buildings are the stilted products of architects who practice rule as a mechanical formula. On the other hand, when anarchy prevails, the results may be delightful but never classical. The Spanish colonial church at Tianguistenco de Galeana, for

3.51. (Left) Christoph Dientzenhofer, Castle Church, Smiřice, Czechoslovakia, 1700-13.

3.52. (Center) Kilian Ignaz Dientzenhofer, Sv. František Xaverský, Opařany, Czechoslovakia, 1732. (Courtesy Christian Norberg Schulz.)

3.53. (Right) Nuestra Señora del Buen Suceso, facade, Tianguistenco de Galeana, near Toluca, Mexico, 1755-97. (Photograph from Portoghesi, *Barocco Latino Americano.*)

3.54. Windblown
"Corinthian" capital,
Martyrial complex of St.
Simeon Stylites, Kal' at
Sim'an, Syria, c. A.D. 475.
(Fototeca Unione at the
American Academy in
Rome, F.U. 22427.)

example, conforms more to indigenous values than to classical rule (fig. 3.53).[51] The details of its facade may be based on the plates of Guarino Guarini's treatise, but the composition adapts more to the Spanish Churrigueresque and the pre-Columbian aesthetic than to the classical tradition.[52]

A capital from the fifth-century A.D. church at Kal' at Sim'an in Syria is another illustration of the collapse of classical values (fig. 3.54).[53] When compared to the Pantheon Corinthian, the windblown capital resembles the paradigm, but its spiky leaves respond to the Byzantine, not classical, aesthetic. Looking beyond the capital, the trabeated relationship between the column and the architrave is replaced with an arch that springs directly from the abacus. A pilaster from the Romanesque cloister of St. Guilhem le Désert in Southern France also demonstrates how the decorative motifs of the classical tradition continued to serve as models despite the breakdown of the Vitruvian concepts of rule and syntax (fig. 3.55). Both structures are medieval buildings that perpetuated memories of classical elements, such as the Corinthian capital, for 1,000 years until the reconstitution of the Vitruvian framework in the Renaissance (fig. 3.56).

3.55. Corinthian pilaster, capital and impost from the cloister of St. Guilhem le Désert, Hérault, France, c. 1200. (The Metropolitan Museum of Art, the Cloisters Collection, purchase 1925; 25.120, 97, 119, 120, 50-51.)

3.56. Carlo Maderno, Corinthian pilaster capital, Santa Susanna, Rome, 1603.

BUILDING CLASSICAL ARCHITECTURE

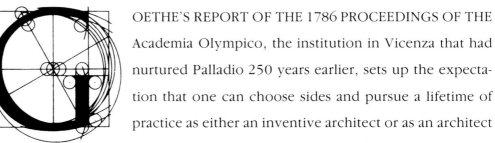

OETHE'S REPORT OF THE 1786 PROCEEDINGS OF THE Academia Olympico, the institution in Vicenza that had nurtured Palladio 250 years earlier, sets up the expectation that one can choose sides and pursue a lifetime of practice as either an inventive architect or as an architect bound to rule. From his own work, Goethe undoubtedly recognized that one should not attempt to neutralize the inherent conflict between rule and invention. The ongoing interchange between these concepts keeps classical architecture alive while maintaining its link to the past.

In the early 1970s I visited all of Palladio's buildings on a pilgrimage to Vicenza to cement my commitment to study architecture. As a student, my projects incorporated the lessons learned from Palladio only in allusive ways. Upon graduation I began to incorporate classical elements in a series of hypothetical projects for houses. These early forays into the world of classical architecture met with various responses. Even supporters called them subversive, and the more loudly critics complained that the classical language was bereft of meaning, the more I realized its potency.

The practice of classical architecture continues to be controversial because it reveals values that contradict the assumptions of our time. The shared experience of painters and composers confirms the missionary role that a number of classical architects share today. As I have moved from initial use of fragments of classical motifs to a position in which wholeness is the ideal, I am increasingly aware of the conceptual gap that separates us from the modernist mentality.

I began to learn the canons for detail and building types in my first classical designs. As my interest and capacity with *regula* increased, some thought that

Monroe House, Lafayette, California, 1986. Doric portico of living room wing with allegorical figures of Rule and Invention painted in the tympanum.

it would quelch the spontaneity of my earlier attempts. These cautions were motivated by a reaction against learning from the past—as though invention was a product of ignorance rather than sophistication. These worries were often accompanied by the suggestion that I incorporate obvious aspects of twentieth-century technology with the "ancient" forms—just to avoid confusion. The anxiety that classical architecture be brought "up to date" must be avoided; its most harmful expression is in the cynical ironies of postmodernism—jokes that often serve as a psychological escape valve to release the tension of architects unwilling to confront classicism at full value.

The alternative is to commit oneself to a lifelong study with standards so high that self-satisfaction is by no means guaranteed. This does not require one to be humorless or "bound by the shackles of symmetry." If we steer the difficult course between rule and invention and find a syntax within the classical language we can express our own vision.

My work is presented here in chronological order. It shows a progressive assimilation of rule and constant experiment with invention. The later examples, like the Doric portico of the Monroe House, show a composure that I have begun to accomplish.

This design employs the Doric canon presented in chapter 2 and conforms to the tetrastyle-type of Doric temple surveyed in chapter 3 (figs. 3.5-3.9). Two allegorical figures in the pediment represent rule and invention.[2] The women sit with clasped hands back-to-back against a Corinthian column, a symbol of the regeneration of classicism. On the right, Invention holds an effigy of Artemis of Ephesus, a symbol of the fertility of ideas. At her feet a mother bear licks the breath of life into her newborn cub, another symbol of invention. On the other side, Rule holds a laurel wreath next to an open book on her lap. The lion at her feet represents authority, and the baboon symbolizes wisdom. These personifications represent the forces that animate classical architecture. In response to Goethe's question, "which has been of greater benefit to the Arts?" we must respond—both!

SUNNYSIDE STREET HOUSE, Oakland, California, 1975

Fig. 4.0a. The Serliana arch motif is the sole classical element of a scheme that attempts to bring a number of formal systems together. The volumetric and spatial exaggeration of Moore and Venturi provided the context for combining Wrightian and Shingle Style elements in addition to the germ of classical vocabulary.

Fig. 4.0b. Interior of dining entry and inglenook toward library.

JEFFERSON STREET HOUSE
Berkeley, California, 1976

Figs. 4.1abc. The three stories of this small house are divided into two volumes. The living room occupies the front. The rear of the ground floor accommodates the dining room and kitchen. Two bedrooms and a bath are on the second level. A bedroom with a balconied loggia is on the third floor.

Although the house is entered from the street, the interior is oriented toward a southern pergola-covered terrace and a garden enclosed by a wall and a grove of trees.

The sloping roof of the living room is left open above the stair to provide a spacious, light-filled entry. The inglenook can be closed off with sliding doors to retain the heat of the double fireplace.

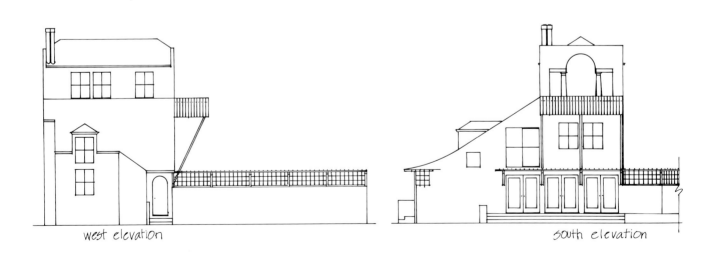

west elevation

south elevation

livingroom and foyer with diningroom beyond

Fig. 4.1d. Plan:

1. ENTRY

2. INGLENOOK—LIVING ROOM

3. DINING ROOM

4. KITCHEN

5. BEDROOM 1

6. BEDROOM 2

7. BEDROOM 3

DORIC HOUSE
Berkeley, California, 1976

Fig. 4.2a. Doric House exaggerates the tension between the classical and vernacular forms latent in Jefferson Street House. Doric columns support an arch articulated with voussoirs formed by layering long shingles.

The cornice melds with the overhang of a California bungalow, the prototype of an economical residence. Both components are bound together by a string course consisting of a Doric architrave and taenia.

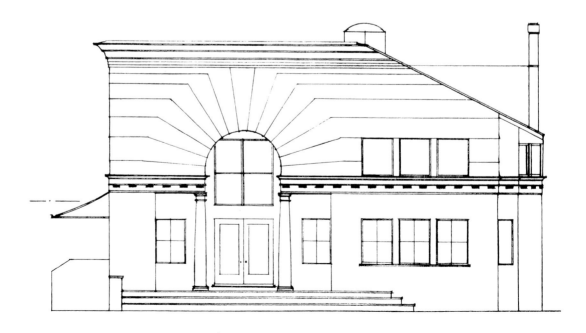

Fig. 4.2b. Elevation.

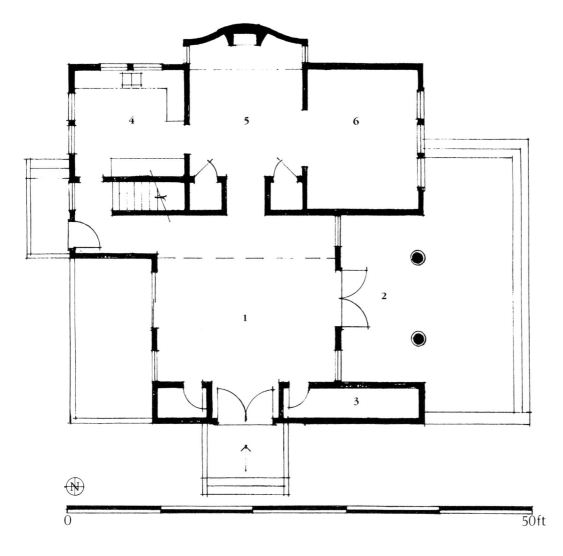

Fig. 4.2c. Plan:
1. LIVING ROOM
2. PORTICO
3. LIBRARY
4. KITCHEN
5. DINING ROOM
6. STUDY

0   50ft

Fig. 4.2d. Interior

IONIC HOUSE
Tagachang
Beach, Guam,
1976

Fig. 4.3a. The living
room of Ionic House is
distinguished by the
baroque form of its
plan. The columns that
support its arched
openings are capped
with glazed terra-cotta
Ionic capitals devel-
oped from the form of
the thun shell.

Fig. 4.3b. Ionic House
is a project for a spec-
tacular palisade over-
looking the Pacific
Ocean. The warm and
humid climatic condi-
tions encourage a
loosely jointed arrange-
ment of rooms. Walls
are replaced by jalousie
louvres that can be
closed off during
typhoons by metal roll-
ing doors.

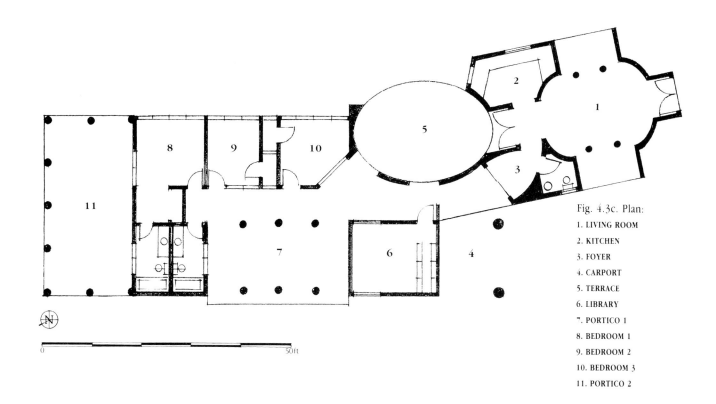

Fig. 4.3c. Plan:
1. LIVING ROOM
2. KITCHEN
3. FOYER
4. CARPORT
5. TERRACE
6. LIBRARY
7. PORTICO 1
8. BEDROOM 1
9. BEDROOM 2
10. BEDROOM 3
11. PORTICO 2

0   50ft

Fig. 4.3d. The bedrooms surround a deep portico spanned by wooden trusses supported by betel-nut palm trunks. These tropical trees grow with a graceful swelling that approximates the entasis of classical columns.

Fig. 4.3e. The use of classical motifs is tempered by the indigenous buildings of Guam. The low-slung proportions, hipped corrugated iron roofs, and the concrete block walls stained ochre-red from the earth pigments resemble the vernacular "boonie" huts of the island.

**RICHARD LONG
HOUSE I
Carson City,
Nevada, 1977**

Fig. 4.4a. The Richard Long House was planned for a majestic site with views of the mountainous landscape in all directions. Three designs were developed, designated Long I, II, III. Each is a variation on the same basic program, materials, and massing. An oval terrace is surrounded by three functional blocks: a formal area, a kitchen and family area, and a bedroom zone. An elevated ''aeroplane'' room provides a panoramic view. (Note: all drawings for Long I, II, III are in the Duetsches Architekturmuseum collection.)

Fig. 4.4b. A perspective view cuts through the dining room and foyer to show the spatial variety of this wing. The curved stair ascends to the aeroplane room and contributes to the sinuous pattern of movement from the entry to the terrace.

The dining room and living room orient toward a southern view and a column screens the inglenook and defines the oval shape of its plan.

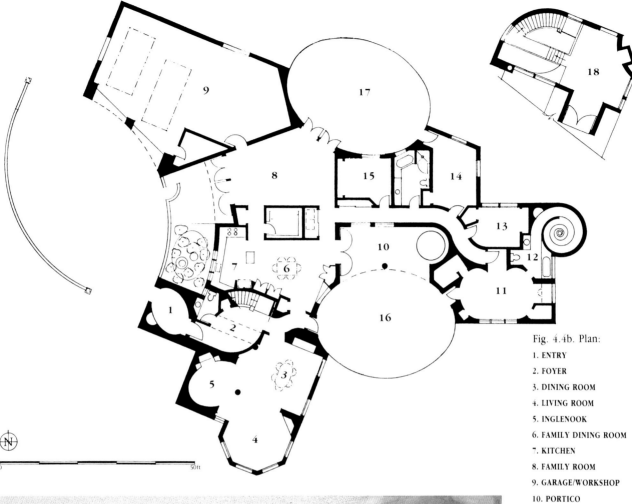

Fig. 4.4b. Plan:

1. ENTRY
2. FOYER
3. DINING ROOM
4. LIVING ROOM
5. INGLENOOK
6. FAMILY DINING ROOM
7. KITCHEN
8. FAMILY ROOM
9. GARAGE/WORKSHOP
10. PORTICO
11. BEDROOM 1
12. SHOWER
13. BEDROOM 2
14. BEDROOM 3
15. BEDROOM 4
16. SOUTH TERRACE
17. NORTH TERRACE
18. AEROPLANE ROOM

Fig. 4.4d. The living and bedroom wings are positioned around the terrace in response to views and in reaction to severe winds that blow from the northwest. The exterior responds to the landscape with a gently curving silhouette that was meant to fulfill the client's initial desire for a house that "rises from lower slopes to mountain peaks."

The desert sagebrush grows up to the perimeter of the house, and gardens are restricted to courtyards. The exterior is sheathed with concrete block of silvery pastel tones to harmonize with the dominant colors of the site: sage, sand, and sky.

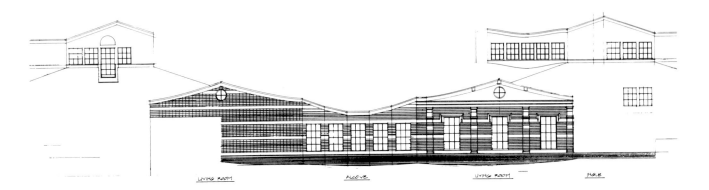

**LONG HOUSE II
Carson City,
Nevada, 1978**

Fig. 4.5a. A developed elevation shows all curved and angled walls of the second Long project stretched out flat. These drawings show the relationship of complex volumes in two dimensions and illustrate the transition from one texture and color of concrete block to another.

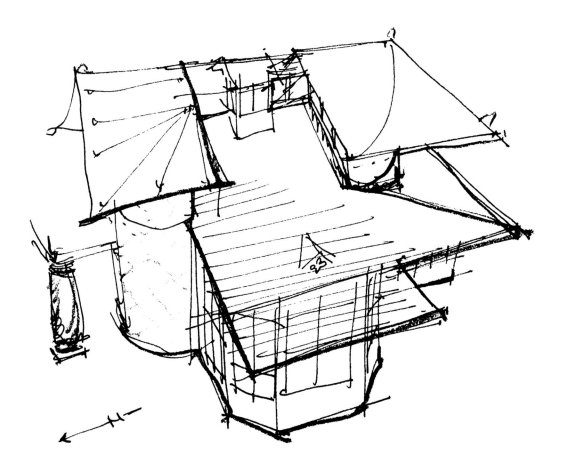

Fig. 4.5b. An aerial sketch of the living room wing is an early study of volumes and roof forms.

Fig. 4.5c. The second Long design reinterprets the volume of the first scheme with broad overhanging roofs and a greater use of classical motifs.

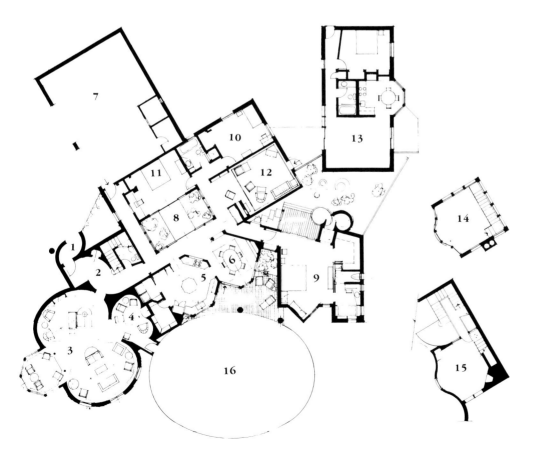

Fig. 4.5d. Plan:

1. ENTRY
2. FOYER
3. LIVING ROOM
4. INGLENOOK
5. KITCHEN
6. DINING ROOM
7. GARAGE/WORKSHOP
8. COURTYARD
9. BEDROOM 1
10. BEDROOM 2
11. BEDROOM 3
12. FAMILY ROOM
13. IN-LAW UNIT
14. STUDY
15. AEROPLANE ROOM
16. SOUTH TERRACE

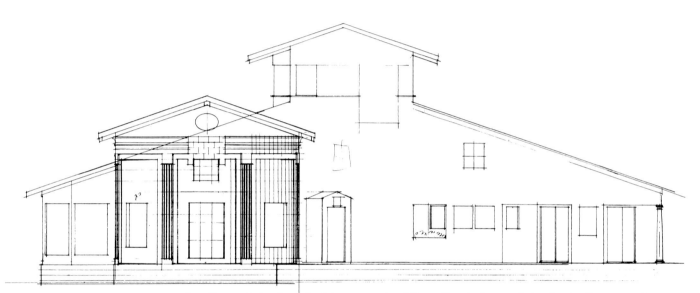

Fig. 4.5e. The south facade of the living room wing follows Vitruvius's prescription for the Tuscan temple. This adaptation responds to the curve of the living room wall. The columns are represented by rusticated concrete block pilasters. The normally wide overhang of the Tuscan temple is exaggerated by the contraction of the wall. After seeing the sheer parapets of the first scheme, the client requested these overhanging eaves because he associated them with a "homelike" quality.

Fig. 4.5f. The northwest side of the living room has no windows due to weather conditions and a need for privacy. A cabinet for the display of Indian artifacts is indirectly illuminated from a clerestory above the ceiling vault. The cabinet is flanked by a tromp-d'oeil painting from the House of Livia in Rome. As in the ancient example, the shadows cast by the structure are painted on the wall. The slender columns represented in the Livia painting are depicted as though they support the arched entry to the alcove.

**LONG HOUSE III
Carson City,
Nevada, 1979**

Fig. 4.6a. This sketch is the genesis of the third version of the Long House. Although the interjection of prefabricated quonset-type buildings was an unacceptable substitute for more conventional construction, the differentiation of pavilions and the reduction of size became the hallmarks of the project.

Fig. 4.6b. A sketch completed further along in the development shows the reuse of previous images, an experiment with an oval aeroplane room, and the placement of a spa enclosure terminating the latitudinal axis of the living room.

105

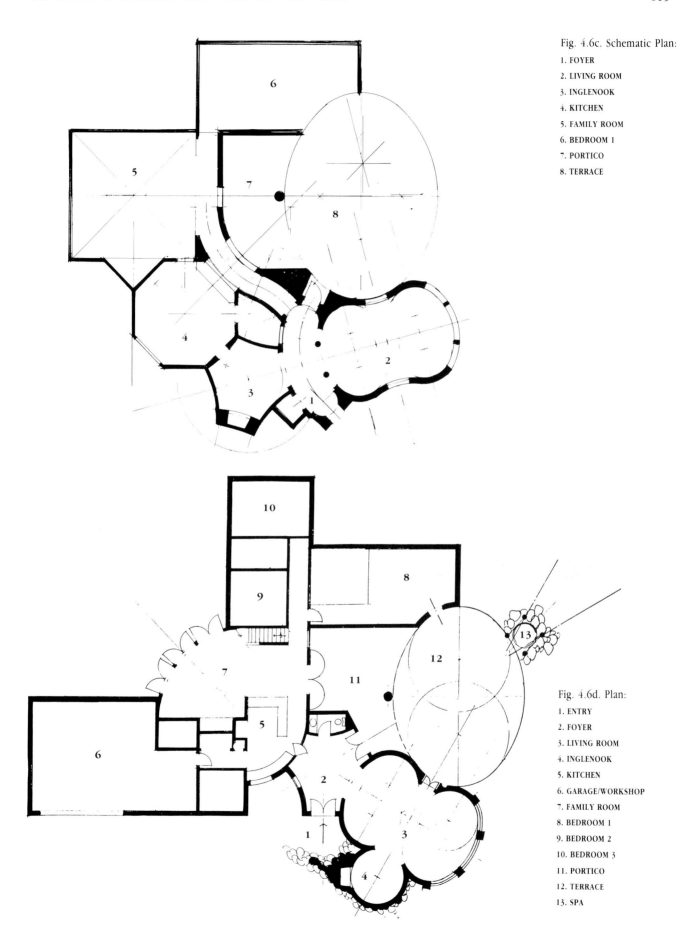

Fig. 4.6c. Schematic Plan:
1. FOYER
2. LIVING ROOM
3. INGLENOOK
4. KITCHEN
5. FAMILY ROOM
6. BEDROOM 1
7. PORTICO
8. TERRACE

Fig. 4.6d. Plan:
1. ENTRY
2. FOYER
3. LIVING ROOM
4. INGLENOOK
5. KITCHEN
6. GARAGE/WORKSHOP
7. FAMILY ROOM
8. BEDROOM 1
9. BEDROOM 2
10. BEDROOM 3
11. PORTICO
12. TERRACE
13. SPA

Fig. 4.6e. The two versions of the plan tightly interrelate the geometrical forms of the second scheme. The elements are arranged without regard to a symmetrical whole on this open, wild site.

The Maybeck-like living room wing incorporates the monumental portal of Michelangelo in opposition to the independent, almost vernacular, structure of the bedroom wing. The aeroplane room is more isolated than in the previous projects.

Fig. 4.6f. The Tuscan temple form is employed at a reduced scale in the living room wing. Concrete block piers rest on a socle buttressed by boulders half buried in the earth. Similar rough stones cascade from the chimney and form a wind protection barrier required at the point of entry.

**PAULOWNIA
HOUSE
Oakland,
California, 1977**

Fig. 4.7a. The shell of this small house is a quonset-type prefabricated building manufactured for agricultural use. The design was an experiment in using an economical industrial material to achieve a vaulted structure. The particular unit is a vault open on three sides for light and ventilation.

At the entry, half of an arch is built perpendicular to a mirrored wall. Reflected it gives the illusion of an entire arch.

Fig. 4.7b. The paulownia crest, a motif of Japanese heraldry, is used throughout the design as a decorative motif.

Fig. 4.7c. The bedroom has a raised tatami sleeping platform that opens onto a wooden deck. A raked sand garden with a planting of paulownia saplings is enclosed by masonry walls and a small bathhouse. This enclosed garden and the other projections from the prefabricated shell fit within the setbacks of a small triangular lot.

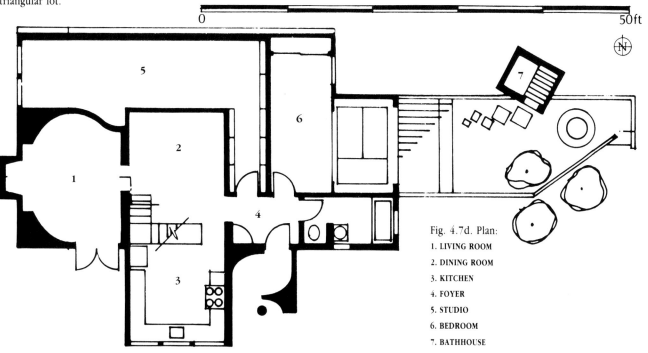

Fig. 4.7d. Plan:

1. LIVING ROOM
2. DINING ROOM
3. KITCHEN
4. FOYER
5. STUDIO
6. BEDROOM
7. BATHHOUSE

SHELL HOUSE
Kensington,
California, 1978

Fig. 4.8a. A sketch project for a small residence on a site adjacent to Bernard Maybeck's 1938 Wallen Maybeck House is developed with two quonset structure pavilions. The front portion follows the form of Palladio's Villa Foscari, in which an Ionic portico projects from the boxlike form of the villa. The portico of Shell House is composed of a segmental arched pediment that follows the curve of the roof. It is supported by Doric columns and an abbreviated entablature.

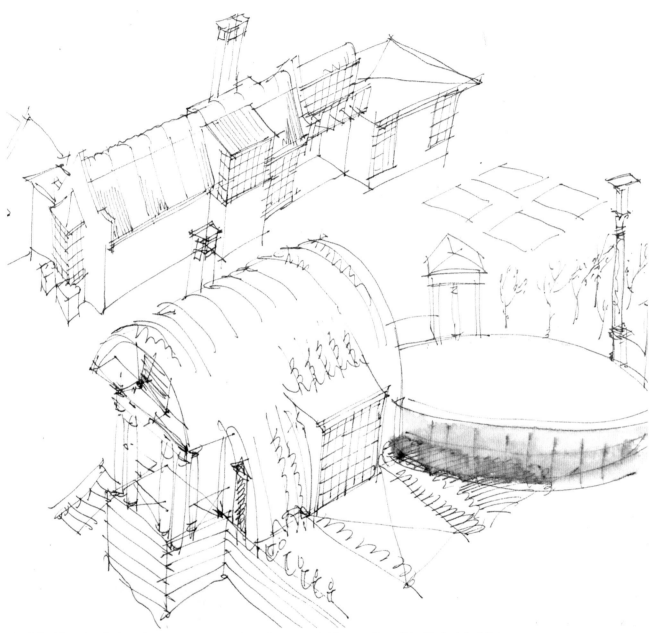

Fig. 4.8b. The galvanized steel structure corresponds to the corrugated iron roofing of the Maybeck building. The front element contains the living room, dining room, and kitchen. The rear unit was planned for bedrooms and baths.

**MATHEWS STREET HOUSE
Berkeley, California, 1978**

Fig. 4.9a. This house was originally planned as a short section of a wide span quonset building. The blank sides were oriented to face the street with the openings oriented north and south. Toward the south a foyer and hall were planned as a light-filled three-story volume into which the bedroom windows would open.

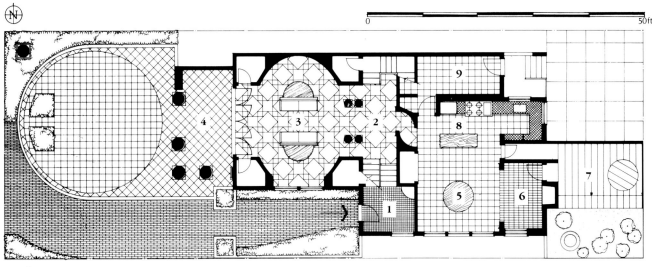

Fig. 4.9b. Plan

1. FOYER
2. HALL
3. LIVING ROOM
4. PORTICO
5. FAMILY DINING ROOM
6. INGLENOOK
7. COVERED DECK
8. KITCHEN
9. LAUNDRY

Fig. 4.9c. The living room pavilion is developed as a brilliant temple form that projects from a simple towerlike mass. The portico is supported by four Doric columns and the anta extension of a wall. The asymmetrical facade captures sun from the southwest and obscures the portico from a neighboring house. The entablature and pediment are adapted from Michelangelo's portal at the top of the *ricetto* stair at the Laurentian Library in Florence (fig. 3.25). The bright Greek polychromy of red and blue is muted by the softer coloration of Bernard Maybeck's palette of peach, ochre, and Chinese green. The boukrania on the metopes are cow skulls. Although many functions have been proposed for the column that stands in front of the house, its intent is purely monumental. It stands in contrast to the Doric portico to indicate the spectrum of the orders, and it signifies the potential for the regeneration of classical architecture typical of the Corinthian (Collection, Deutsches Architekturmuseum).

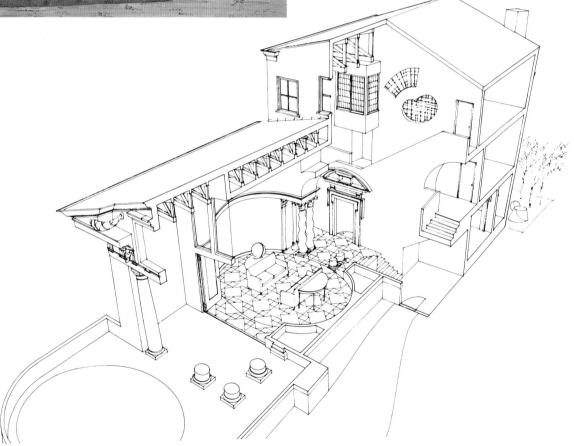

Fig. 4.9d. As the design evolved into a more conventional wood frame building, the three-story hall was oriented west and became a center for circulation. Its source of light was changed to high clerestory windows that resemble a nineteenth-century Japanese tea merchant's town house reconstructed at Meiji-mura, Japan.

The living room and portico form a unit which is separate from the more utilitarian block that contains a kitchen and informal family areas on the first floor and bedrooms and bathrooms above (Collection, Deutsches Architekturmuseum).

**TUSCAN HOUSE
AND LAUREN-
TIAN HOUSE
Livermore,
California, 1979**

Fig. 4.10a. The Tuscan House faces the street with the broad, gabled form of the Tuscan temple. This conveys a sense of simplicity in contrast to the brighter polychromy of the triumphal arch entry to the Laurentian House.

Fig. 4.10b. These adjacent houses were designed to convey the sense of place and character evoked in two letters written by Pliny describing his Tuscan and Laurentian villas. Tuscan and Laurentian houses are not attempts at reconstruction, but they reflect the ambiance of Pliny's villas and of Mediterranean houses in general.

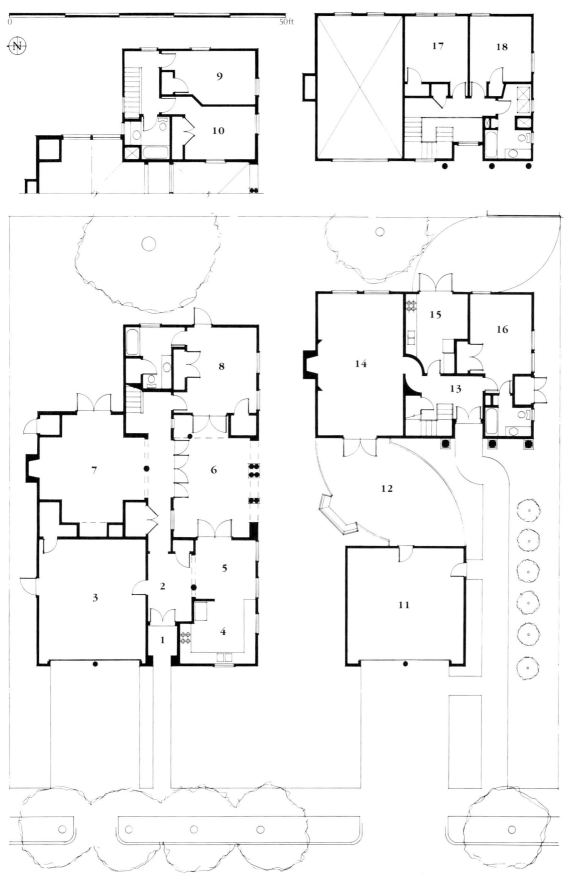

1. ENTRY
2. FOYER
3. GARAGE
4. KITCHEN
5. DINING AREA
6. COURT
7. LIVING ROOM
8. BEDROOM 1
9. BEDROOM 2
10. BEDROOM 3

11. GARAGE
12. PIAZZETTA
13. FOYER
14. LIVING ROOM
15. KITCHEN
16. BEDROOM 1
17. BEDROOM 2
18. BEDROOM 3

Fig. 4.10c. **Tuscan House Plan**   **Laurentian House Plan**

Fig. 4.10de. Like the Doric and Mathews Street houses, the three columns and Doric entablature of the Laurentian entryway create a contradiction between the expectation of a symmetrical composition within an asymmetrical context. This facade and the Laurentian garage create a piazzetta that brings sunlight to the court and living room of Tuscan House.

Fig. 4.10fghi; The cruciform living room of Tuscan House is patterned after the Greek cross-shaped *salone* of Palladio's Villa Foscari. It is illuminated by windows on three sides, and it is painted white in contrast to the bright exterior colors to promote the reflection of light. The faceted ceiling articulates its shape and indicates its hierarchical importance in the house.

**FACADE DEDICATED TO
ARCHITETTURA
Strada Novissima,
Venice Biennale, 1980**

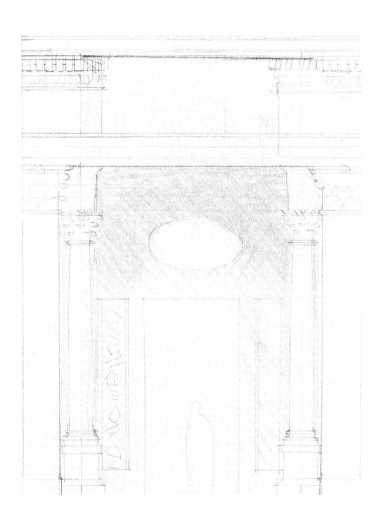

Fig. 4.11a. In the late 1970s Paolo Portoghesi
devised the idea to hold an international show of
architecture as part of the biennial exhibition of
art in Venice. "The Presence of the Past" was the
theme for 1980. Twenty architects were invited to
design facades erected to form two sides of a
street along the interior of a former rope-making
factory in the Venice Arsenal. This group of structures and the exhibitions of seventy architects
demonstrated the growing receptivity to learning
from the history of architecture. My schematic
design for the facade contained a pair of small
columns surrounded by a giant order of pilasters,
executed as Doric rather than Corinthian. The contrast between Doric and Corinthian expresses the
contrasts of character within the spectrum of the
orders.

Fig. 4.11bc. In the completed facade the smaller order is developed as a pair of Solomonic Corinthian columns. They project from a concave wall to create a shallow apse around the Ionic portal. Allegorical figures of *Architettura* and *Disegno* are painted on one side of the pediment opposite their antithesis, *Errore*. The ideas expressed by their human attributes and physical stance project a more precise sense of character than the architectural components can.

**ORATORY OF
ST. JEAN
VIANNEY
Rome, 1980**

ORATORY OF ST. JEAN VIANNEY
Rome, 1980

Fig. 4.12ab. An oratory to foster the revival of preaching was designed during my stay at the American Academy in Rome. It meets the liturgical and spiritual requirements of a contemporary church. John Beldon Scott developed an iconographic program based on a dedication and functional program provided by the Reverend George Rutler. St. Jean-Baptiste Marie Vianney was a parish priest in Southern France around the turn of the nineteenth century. Despite many disabilities, his capacity as a charismatic orator and confessor made him the patron of parish priests.

The project site is a vacant triangle of land at the northern end of the Via Giulia, the first street of Rome to have been straightened and rebuilt during the Renaissance. The site is adjacent to a derelict convent dedicated to St. Filippo Neri (1), designed in the eighteenth century by Filippo Raguzzini. The oratory (2) is entered from a small piazza (3) at the end of Via Monserrato. The Oratory's spherical volume is centered on the triangular site. A Star of David inlayed on its circular floor represents the theological foundation on which the church rests and is oriented to emphasize three liturgical axes. The Eucharistic axis begins in the sacristy (4), passes through the altar (5) and presbytery (6), and terminates in the Eucharistic chapel (7). The penitential axis begins in the ambulatory (8) and ends in the octagonal baptistry with its confessionals (9). The public enters the oratory from a vestibule (10) on axis with the pulpit (11).

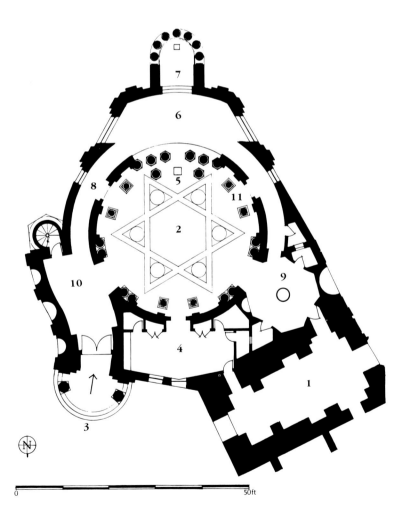

Fig. 4.12cde. A sepia
sketch shows the
schematic development
of the exterior of the
Oratory. The prowlike
form of the Eucharistic
chapel projects toward
the Via Giulia. The
facade to the left main-
tains the two-
dimensional format of
palaces along the street.
To the right, the tower
is crowned by the bell
that Vianney mounted
to initiate the revitaliza-
tion of his derelict
church at Ars. The
arches of the pres-
bytery are filled with
stained-glass windows
depicting angels wres-
tling with the instru-
ments of the Passion
(Collection, John Bel-
don Scott).

Fig. 4.12f. The interior of the Oratory is composed
of two spherical volumes. The larger one is
defined by the earthy container of a dome supported by Tuscan and Doric columns. Within this,
three pairs of marble Solomonic columns support
ogival vaults to form an ethereal baldacchino. One
pair of these columns form an aedicula around the
pulpit. A statue of the orator's mentor, St. Jean
Vianney, hovers above. Both preacher and effigy
aspire toward the third zone, a stained glass window that depicts an emblem of Divine Wisdom
(Collection, Deutsches Architekturmuseum).

RICHMOND HILL HOUSE
Richmond, California, 1983

Fig. 4.13a. Richmond Hill House is approached through a court surrounded by plants cultivated in ancient Roman gardens. The foyer is the only public area on the first floor; beyond this bedrooms and bathrooms occupy the first level. A stair leads to the kitchen/dining room and living room on the second floor. They were located at the higher level to obtain maximum light and to glimpse views of the San Francisco Bay. Because of the narrow width of the house, these rooms have windows on three sides. A playroom is located under the slope of the roof above the kitchen. (All photographs of Richmond Hill House are by Henry Bowles.)

The words of a poem by Thomas d'Urfey, put to song in 1692 by Henry Purcell, are painted as an inscription around the living room frieze:

*On the brow
Of Richmond
  Hill
which Europe
  scarce
can parallel
ev'ry eye
such wonders
  fill
to view the
prospect round
where the
silver Thames
doth glide
and stately
  courts
are edified.*

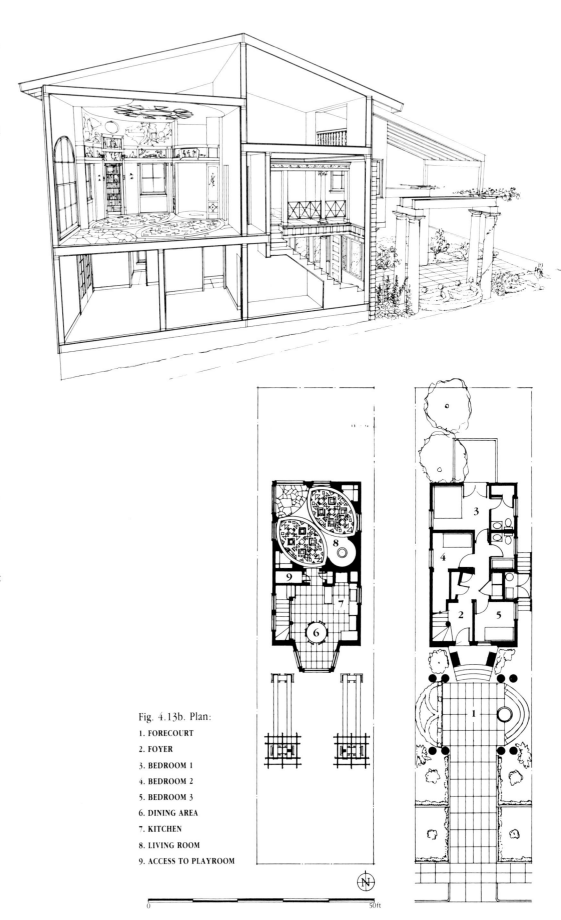

Fig. 4.13b. Plan:

1. FORECOURT
2. FOYER
3. BEDROOM 1
4. BEDROOM 2
5. BEDROOM 3
6. DINING AREA
7. KITCHEN
8. LIVING ROOM
9. ACCESS TO PLAYROOM

0   50ft

Fig. 4.13c. The house faces south on a narrow lot. A trellis extends from the roof and rests on eight Doric columns to enclose a forecourt. The columns are spanned by a rudimentary entablature, and boukrania hang between the triglyphs. Limestone is affixed to the walls of the house and marble pilasters surround the door.

Fig. 4.13fi. The colors of the house reflect the light differently, whether in full sun or in the evening when atmospheric conditions infuse the palette with greater intensity.

Fig. 4.13degh. The living room is symmetrical about a diagonal axis that originates in a niche for a harpsichord. The tight curve of this nook is reinforced by concave walls, that create spatial movement contradicting the rectilinearity of the rest of the house. Oval patterns of the floor contribute to the sense of flux, and their tinted concrete matrix contains a geometrical pattern of pieces of marble. The walls and ceiling are plastered and finished with a coat of polished lampblack and marble dust, following the ancient Roman fresco technique. The paintings have two themes: the passage of time and homage to oil, Richmond's primary industry. Four groups of figures illustrate the myth of Persephone to indicate the cycle of the year. The southern quadrant of the room depicts winter. Demeter, the mother of the abducted Persephone, scours the earth in search of her daughter. Hermes tries to placate her and is shown in a subsequent negotiation with the abductor, Hades, and Persephone—a meeting that wins her partial freedom.

On the ceiling, the nine ages of man and woman are shown from conception through death. At the center of this cycle Petrolia, a twentieth-century allegorical figure, gazes toward the distant oil refineries.

Below the mythical figures, an architectural armature is decorated with the products of each season's garden. As in Pompeiian examples, birds inhabit this region. In this case, birds were chosen to represent the character of the ages. The kingfisher stands for a mature man and the lyrebird represents a young man's adolescence. Small vignettes painted on four black wall panels convey a final indication of passage of time and allude to oil. The Romans painted vignettes of shrines surrounded by supplicants and landscape features on walls like these. At Richmond these are reinterpreted as eight gas stations, one for each decade of this century.

MASTER PLANNING FOR LONE MOUNTAIN
San Francisco, California, 1984

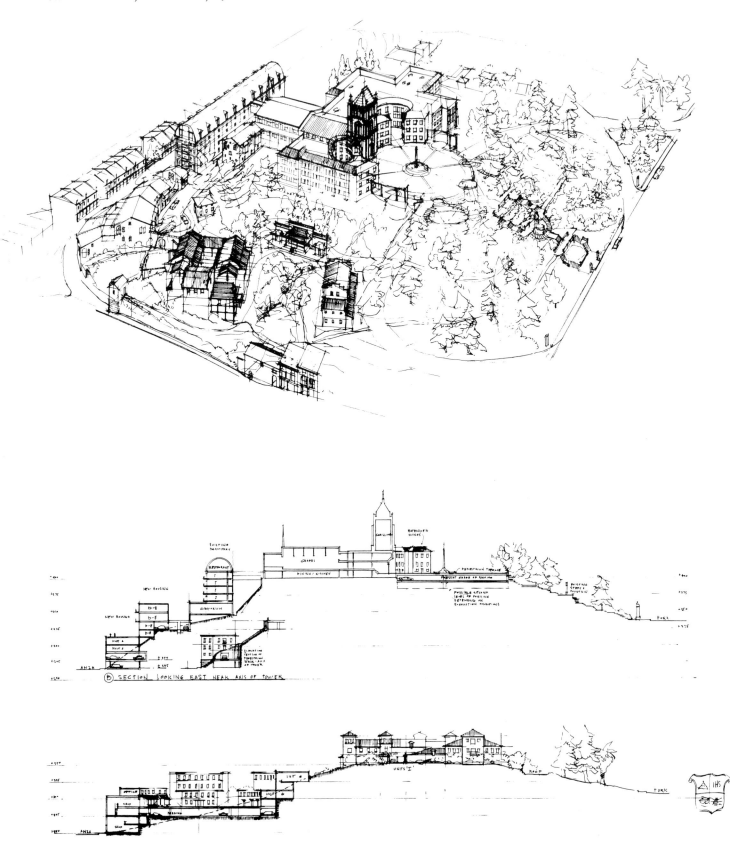

Figs. 4.14abcd. This master planning project for the site of a Jesuit college campus in San Francisco entails additions to the existing college buildings, the remodeling of a dormitory into studio condominiums, four sectors of private houses, commercial buildings, and a Buddhist monastery. The project sprang from the idea to create houses that could be a source of endowment for the university but which would also create a community of nonstudents who could use the resources of the existing campus buildings for cultural events.

The existing neo-Gothic tower at the top of Lone Mountain is flanked by new wings to form a circular piazza. This provides a vista point for one of San Francisco's most prominent hills and creates a special place for Lone Mountain. At the center of the piazza, a fountain represents the source of the four rivers presented in the Genesis narrative. From this fountain, water is sent out in the cardinal directions and divides the site into quadrants. Each of these streams takes on a unique character. The southern direction amplifies the supply of an existing fountain found in an axial Spanish Steps stairway. The eastern and western streams take on a more natural form, developing a Chinese garden below the monastery to the west and a secluded brook for the most exclusive group of houses to the east.

The steep slope to the north is developed with a dense urban group of town houses and commercial facilities. The existing dormitory is converted to studio apartments which increase the density. On the north the water gushes out from under the bank of the dormitory tower to feed a cascade of fountains dividing into three ranges of terraced stairs. The dormitory is faced with superposed orders of pilasters to break down its stark mass. The houses are rendered in a restrained Mediterranean classical manner and are tightly clustered to reflect the density of the adjacent urban areas while maintaining existing open space.

The Buddhist monastery is modeled on an example from China and is located in one of the existing park-like areas. Its colored stucco walls and tile roofs, although authentic to the Chinese example, relate to the Mediterranean buildings in the nearby residences. The orientation of the monastery follows the *Feng Shui*, or system of sacred orientation, found in the Chinese prototype.

SHRINE TO APOLLO AND DAPHNE
Deutsches Architekturmuseum, Frankfurt, 1984

Fig. 4.15abcd. This garden court provided an opportunity to explore the notion of character in the orders. The court is a shrine dedicated to Apollo on the site of Daphne's metamorphosis into a laurel tree. A Corinthian column contrasts with the Doricism of the existing ashlar walls and supports a pergola

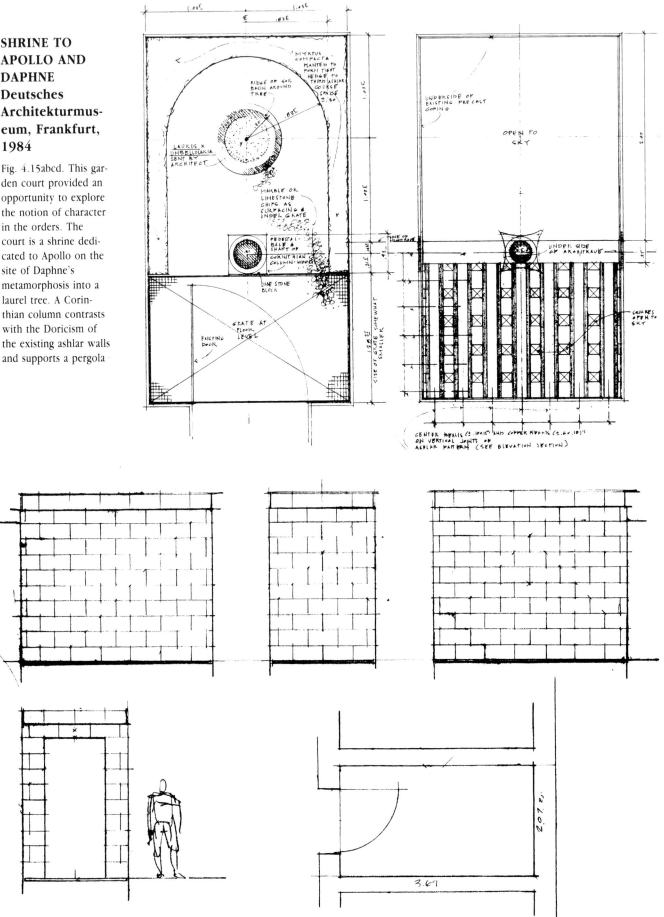

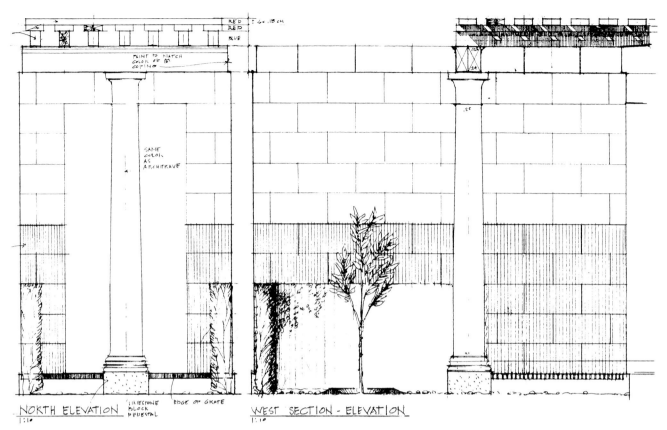

RED
RED
BLUE

PAINT TO MATCH
COLOR OF (B)
COPING

SAME
COLOR
AS
ARCHITRAVE

NORTH ELEVATION
1:10

LIMESTONE
BLOCK
PEDESTAL

EDGE OF GRATE

WEST SECTION - ELEVATION
1:10

Fig. 4.15e. The capital is a variation on the first architectural development of the Corinthian order at Bassae. Laurel leaves are used instead of the second register of acanthus. A bronze flame replaces the volute to represent Apollo's fiery side. His dual sensibility is conveyed by the acanthus and the flamelike laurel. Daphne is present in the courtyard as the sacred laurel tree itself; in this case, a hybrid of the Mediterranean *Laurus nobilis* and the California bay laurel (collection, Deutsches Architekturmuseum).

Fig. 4.15f. The first design explores the notion of character in the archaic form of the Doric. The apse is based on the prototype of the Temple of Apollo at Thermon and was designed to have painted terra-cotta metopes depicting the myth of Apollo and Daphne (Collection, Hans Baldauf).

EDGEWOOD DAY TREATMENT CENTER San Francisco, California, 1985

Figs. 4.16abcd. This addition to a day school for emotionally disturbed children reinforces the character of an existing Renaissance-style building constructed in 1924 as an orphanage dormitory. Adding a classroom and administrative wing to the structure presented an opportunity to relate the new and old portions in a hierarchical arrangement. The existing building is not shown in the renderings, but the addition replicates its H-shape in plan to create a courtyard to the south. The two blocks are linked by an administrative wing, the central foyer of which is on the level of the existing structure. The foyer opens to the west with an Ionic portico to emphasize the entry. The podium re-establishes the horizontal register of the socle in the existing building; all elements above this line are Ionic; elements below are Doric.

The classroom wing is one-half level below the foyer. This change in height gives the children direct access to the court and a playground. The parapet walls of this one-story structure convey a simple image that is elevated by the Doric porches and the columnar screen that encloses the courtyard.

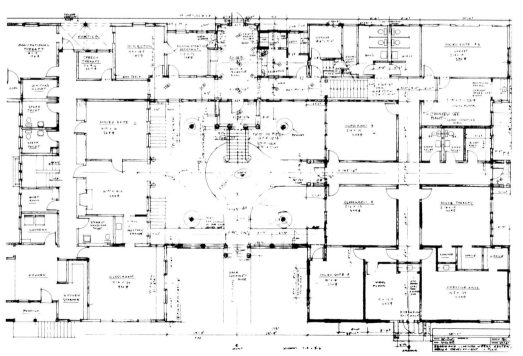

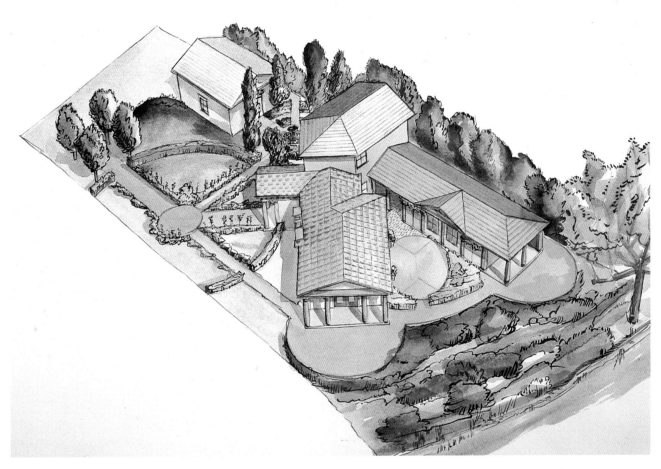

MONROE HOUSE
Lafayette,
California, 1986

Fig. 4.17a. This house is planned for a suburban lot in one of the warm interior valleys of the San Francisco Bay Area. The site is a subdivision of a larger plot with access to the garage from a private drive on the north. The house is oriented away from this access point and toward the steep ravine of a creek toward the south. The volume is broken into three pavilions; a two-story structure anchors two wings projecting to the south and southwest. Each unit is articulated by different orders. The central "tower" has an Ionic entablature. The utility wing to the east is Tuscan and the living room is Doric. The selection of orders corresponds with the general hierarchy of public, private, and utility areas.

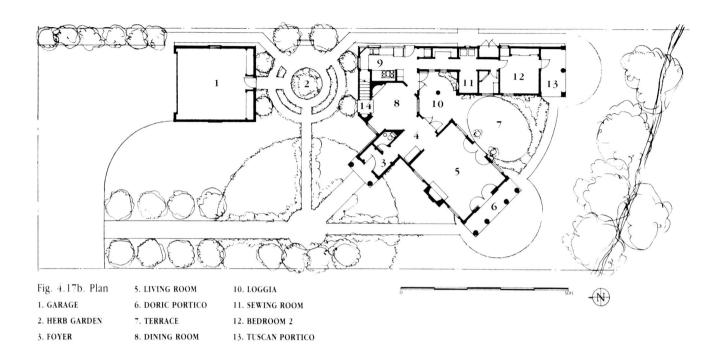

Fig. 4.17b. Plan

1. GARAGE	5. LIVING ROOM	10. LOGGIA
2. HERB GARDEN	6. DORIC PORTICO	11. SEWING ROOM
3. FOYER	7. TERRACE	12. BEDROOM 2
4. HALL	8. DINING ROOM	13. TUSCAN PORTICO
	9. KITCHEN	14. ACCESS TO BEDROOM 1

4.17c. Entablature detail.

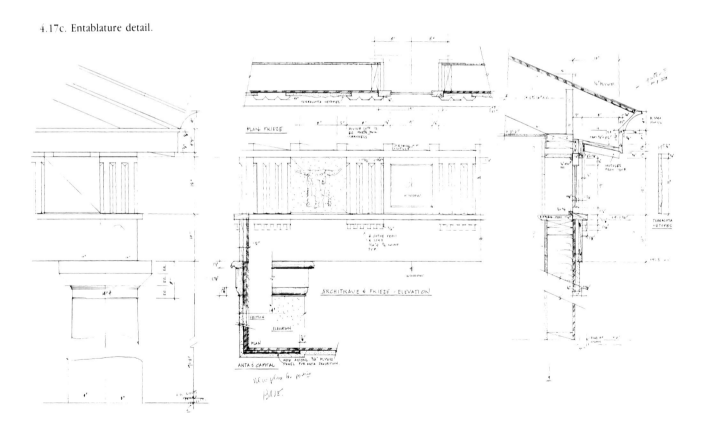

Fig. 4.17d. A view from the southwest shows the herb garden located between the garage and the two-story structure. A fountain designed after a vignette on a Pompeiian fresco is the centerpiece. The entry porch extends from the living room wing and is emphasized by a quarter circular myrtle hedge. The Doric entablature continues around this porch and is cast in relief at the concrete chimney. The polychromy of the entablature highlights its wood detail. The metopes are glazed terra-cotta with decorative reliefs cast on the surface. The roof materials are different for each pavilion. The Doric has a flat "Corinthian" terra-cotta tile, the tower is slate and the low Tuscan wing has a wood shingle roof.

Fig. 4.17e. The courtyard formed by the projecting wings consists of an oval terrace oriented on the transverse axis of the living room. It extends from the irregularly-shaped court where the wings converge and a loggia opens onto it from the kitchen. The climate allows doors and windows to be open for much of the year and encourages outdoor living. The porticoes not only provide the most definite indication of classical architecture but provide outdoor rooms. The Monroe House develops the concepts of character and order through the selection of columns as well as the treatment of volume and material.

BIBLIOGRAPHY

PUBLICATION OF BUILDINGS AND PROJECTS, BY DATE

Gebhard, David, and Susan King. *A View of California Architecture: 1960-1976,* 7, 12, 44, 61. San Francisco: San Francisco Museum of Modern Art, 1976.

Culot, Maurice. "Les Ordres de Thomas Gordon Smith." *Archives d' Architecture Moderne,* no. 12 (Brussels, November 1977): 62-64.

Jencks, Charles. "Genealogy of Post-Modern Architecture." *Architectural Design* 47, no. 4 (London, 1977): 269-271.

Jencks, Charles. *The Language of Post-Modern Architecture,* 129, 132. New York: Rizzoli International, 1977.

Davis, Douglas. "Designs for Living." *Newsweek* 92, no. 19 (November 6, 1978): 89.

Jencks, Charles. "Late Modernism and Post-Modernism." *Architectural Design* 48, no. 11-12 (London 1978): 604, 606-609.

Jencks, Charles. "Post-Modern History." *Architectural Design* 8, no. 1 (London 1978): 56-57.

Smith, Thomas Gordon. "Re-Drawing from Classicism." *The Journal of Architectural Education* 32, no. 1 (September 1978): 17-23.

Allende, Gabriel. "Thomas Gordon Smith." *Arquitectura,* no. 220 (Madrid September-October 1979): 26-27.

Nakamura, Toshio. "Thomas Gordon Smith, Five Projects." *A + U Architecture and Urbanism* 2 (Tokyo, February 1979): 7, 9, 11-14.

Nevins, Deborah, and Robert A. M. Stern. *The Architect's Eye, American Architectural Drawings from 1799-1978,* 18, 164-165. New York: Pantheon Books, 1979.

Bottero, Maria. "Il Postmodernismo alla Biennale di Venezia." *Abitare,* no. 187 (Milan September 1980): 160-210.

D'Arms, John H. "Thomas Smith." *Annual Exhibition.* Rome: American Academy in Rome, 1980.

Jencks, Charles. "Tuscan House and Laurentian House." *Post-Modern Classicism,* 49-52. London: Architectural Design, 1980.

Meccoli, Sandro. "All' Arsenale di Venezia Fiorisce L' Archittetura." *Corriere Della Sera Illustrato,* no. 31 (Rome, August 2, 1980): 16-18.

Radice, Barbara, and Maddalena Sisto. "Il Ritorno delle Colonne." *Casa Vogue,* no. 112 (Milano, November 1980): 222-226.

Smith, Thomas Gordon. "Statement." *The Presence of the Past,* 285-288. Venice: Edizioni La Biennale di Venezia, 1980.

Klotz, Heinrich. "Das 'Laurentianische' und das 'Tuskische' Haus." *Jahrbuch für Architektur 1981-82,* 188-199. Braunschweig/Wiesbaden: Friedr. Vieweg & Sohn 1981.

Kulterman, Udo. "Space, Time and the New Architecture." *A + U,* no. 125 (Tokyo: February 1981): 29.

Malone, Maggie. "Il Kitsch Fatto in Casa." *L' Altro Panorama.* (Rome, 13 April 1981): 16.

Morton, David. "Eclectic Revivals." *Progressive Architecture* (October 1981): 98-101.

Nielsen, Hans Peter Svendler. *Huset som billede,* 59. Denmark: Louisiana Museum, 1981.

Searing, Helen. *Speaking a New Classicism: American Architecture Now,* 48-50. Northampton, Mass.: Smith College Museum of Art, 1981.

Sisto, Maddalena. "Domus Nova in California." *Casa Vogue,* no. 123 (Milan, October 1981): 226-229.

Smith, Thomas Gordon. "Subject in Architecture." *San Francisco Bay Architect's Review,* no. 22 (Winter 1981): 11, 12.

Stern, Robert, A. M. "American Architecture: After Modernism." *A + U* 3 (Tokyo, March 1981): 298-304.

Takeyama, Minoro. "Laurentian House and Tuscan House." *A + U* (Tokyo, 1981): 40-50.

Fujii, Wayne. "Tuscan and Laurentian House, Richmond Hill House." *Global Architecture 10,* 154-161. Tokyo: A.D.A. Edita Tokyo Co., Ltd., 1982.

Haker, Werner. "Matthews Street House, Tuscan House and Laurentian House." *Werk,*

Bauen + Wohnen, no. 5 (Zürich: 1982): 13, 18-19, 28-29.

Harling, Robert. "Inspired by Pliny." *House and Garden* 37, no. 12 (London, December 1982): 108-109.

Jencks, Charles. *Current Architecture.* New York: Rizzoli International, 1982.

—. "Free Style Classicism." *Architectural Design* 52, no. 112 (London 1982): 7, 19.

Jensen, Robert, and Patricia Conway. *Ornamentalism: The New Decorativeness in Architecture and Design.* New York: C. N. Potter, 1982.

King, Carol Soucek. "The Presence of the Past." *Designers West,* 89-94. Los Angeles: Arts Alliance Corp., 1982.

Portoghesi, Paolo. *After Modern Architecture,* 75,89. New York: Rizzoli International, 1982.

Skude, Flemming. "Amerikanske impulser 1976-1981." *Arkitekten,* no. 22 (Copenhagen: Danske Arkitekters Lan ds for bund, November 1982): 445, 449.

Stern, Robert A. M. "Las Duplicidades del Postmodernismo." *Arquitectura,* no. 238 (Madrid, Sept.-Oct. 1982): 26-29, 68-75.

Tigerman, Stanley, and Susan Grant Lewin. *The California Condition, A Pregnant Architecture,* 13, 16, 38, 83-86. La Jolla, California: La Jolla Museum of Contemporary Art, 1982.

Lewin, Susan Grant. "Palladio in America." *House Beautiful* 125, no. 1 (January 1983): 65.

Smith, Thomas Gordon. "Die Gabe des Janus." *Jahrbuch für Architektur, 1983,* 145-150. Braunschweig/Wiesbaden: Friedr. Vieweg & Sohn, 1983.

Smith, Thomas Gordon. "Richmond Hill House." *Oz* 5 (Manhattan, Kansas, 1983): 36-37.

Bergdoll, Barry. "Prototypes and Archetypes." *Architectural Record* (August 1984): 108, 117.

Gebhard, David. "Architecture: Thomas Gordon Smith." *Architectural Digest* (October 1984): 176-181.

Gleiniger-Neumann, Andrea. "Thomas Gordon Smith." *Die Revision der Moderne,* 263-278. Munich: Prestel-Verlag, 1984.

Klotz, Heinrich. *Moderne und Postmoderne, Architektur der Gegenwart 1960-1980,*

202-208. Braunschweig/Wiesbaden: Friedr. Vieweg & Sohn, 1984.

Blodgett, Bonnie. "Model Home." *Ambassador* 18, no. 10 (October 1985): 116.

Fujii, Wayne. "Richmond Hill House." *Global Architecture Houses* [17] (Tokyo, February 1985): 18-23.

Klotz, Heinrich. "Thomas Gordon Smith." *Architectural Design,* no. 55, 3/4 (London, 1985): 58-59.

Smith, Thomas Gordon. "Rule-Invention, Classical Architecture." *Arts & Architecture* (July 1985): 65-69.

Werner, Frank. *Klassizismen und Klassiker,* 45-46. Karlsruhe, West Germany: Badischer Kunstrerein e.v., 1985.

Woodbridge, Sally. "Vest Pocket Villa." *Progressive Architecture* (March 1985): 86-90.

Gebhard, David, Eric Sandweiss, and Robert Winter. *Architecture in San Francisco and Northern California,* cover, 241, 322. Salt Lake City: Gibbs M. Smith, Inc., 1985.

Klotz, Heinrich. *Postmodern Visions: Drawings, Paintings and Models by Contemporary Architects.* New York: Abbeville Press, 1985.

Gleiniger-Neumann, Andrea. *Nouveaux Plaisirs d'Architectures,* 150-151. Paris: Centre Georges Pompidou, 1985.

Stern, Robert A. M. *Current Classicism.* New York: Rizzoli International, 1987.

Tigerman, Stanley. *Literacy and Language.* New York: Rizzoli International, 1987.

NOTES

PREFACE

1. Richard Longstreth, *On the Edge of the World: Four Architects in San Francisco at the Turn of the Century* (New York: The Architectural History Foundation, 1983).

INTRODUCTION

1. G. K. Chesterton, "Eugenics and Other Evils," in *As I Was Saying: A Chesterton Reader*, ed. Robert Knille (Grand Rapids, Mich.: William B. Eerdmans Publishing Co., 1985), p. 272.

2. John James Coulton, *Ancient Greek Architects at Work: Problems of Structure and Design* (Ithaca: Cornell University Press, 1977), pp. 32-50.

3. Coulton, *Ancient Greek Architects at Work*, pp. 55-58. A discussion of *paradigma*.

4. Charles W. Moore, Gerald Allen, and Donlyn Lyndon, *The Place of Houses* (New York: Holt, Rinehart and Winston, 1974).

5. Kenneth H. Cardwell, *Bernard Maybeck: Artisan, Architect, Artist* (Salt Lake City: Peregrine Smith, Inc., 1977), pp. 163-64. Cardwell published the traditional speculation that Maybeck was involved in the preliminary design of the Temple of Wings, but his responsibility is not documented.

The late Sülgwynn Quitzow and her daughter, OEloèl Quitzow Braun, have perpetuated the Isadora Duncan style of dance at the Temple of Wings. OEloèl kindly made the photographs available for publication. Margretta Mitchell has provided much information about the Temple and its original configuration. She has documented the dance activities there since the 1960s, and her photographic portfolio, "Dance for Life," is part of a long-range project to publish photographs and commentary about the house and its traditions.

6. Berkeley resident Sam Hume is credited with coining the phrase "Athens of the West" about 1900, in connection with the construction of John Galen Howard's Greek Theater on the University of California Campus. A parallel, if not so monumental, version of Boynton's ideal of natural living is found in Charles A. Keeler, *The Simple Home* (Salt Lake City: Peregrine Smith, Inc., 1979).

7. Harvey L. Jones, *Mathews: Masterpieces of the California Decorative Style* (Salt Lake City: Gibbs M. Smith, Inc., 1985).

8. Marc-Antoine Laugier, *An Essay on Architecture,* trans. Wolfgang and Anni Herrmann (Los Angeles: Hennessey and Ingalls, Inc., 1977), pp. 11-12. See also Wolfgang Herrmann's discussion of Laugier's ideal building of columns and a roof in *Laugier and Eighteenth Century French Theory* (London: A. Zwemmer, 1962).

9. Conrad Cummings' three-act opera, *Eros and Psyche,* was performed by the Oberlin Opera Theater in November 1983 in celebration of Oberlin College's 150th anniversary. Philippa Kiraly, reviewing the work for the British publication *Opera*, wrote, "The Oracle, whose wordless spiel was imperceptibly taken over by a computer voice, provided a delightfully other-worldly touch. The delineation of character in the music is a strong point of the opera. . . ." The work is dedicated to critic Andrew Porter, who has championed the dramatic revival of baroque opera. Porter was quoted as saying, "The music is very tuneful . . . quite reminiscent of the eighteenth century, though it could not have been written by any eighteenth-century composer." I am grateful to Alan Curtis for putting me in contact with Conrad Cummings in 1983.

10. "David Ligare," *American Artist* (September 1984), pp. 34-39. See also:

Kathy Zimmerer-McKelvie, "The Visual Time Machine: Jon Swihart and David Ligare," *Visual Art* (Summer 1984).

Leon Krier, "Et in Arcadia David Ligare," *Art and Design* (London, November 1986), pp. 40-41. Krier writes, "A great many people are now quite bored with visions à la 'shape of things to come'; if anything the latter have come to mean visions of nightmare rather than of promise. Ligare's landscapes are free of industrial clutter and hysteria."

I thank Janey Bennett for introducing me to David Ligare.

11. The most accessible editions of these treatises are:

Vitruvius, *The Ten Books on Architecture,* trans. Morris Hicky Morgan (1914) (New York: Dover Publications, Inc., 1960). This edition is inexpensive, well bound, and usable despite its amusingly pedantic language.

Vitruvius, *On Architecture,* vols. I and II, trans. Frank Granger (1932) (Cambridge: Harvard University Press, 1962). I am collaborating with philologist Ingrid Rowland to produce a new illustrated and annotated translation of Vitruvius's *Ten Books.*

Andrea Palladio, *The Four Books of Architecture,* trans. Isaac Ware (1738) (New York: Dover Publications, Inc., 1965). Although the translation is clear, the engraved plates lack the warmth of the wood blocks of the original editions which are well reproduced in:

Andrea Palladio, *I Quattro Libri dell'Architettura,* facsimile of the 1570 edition (Milano: Ulrico Hoepli Editore, S.p.A., 1976).

William Chambers, *A Treatise on the Decorative Part of Civil Architecture,* facsimile of the 1791 edition (New York: Benjamin Blom, Inc., 1968).

See Chapter 1, note 17, for additional citations of architectural treatises.

12. Jerome J. Pollitt, *Art and Experience in Classical Greece* (Cambridge: Cambridge University Press, 1976), p. 2.

13. John Summerson, *The Classical Language of Architecture* (Cambridge: MIT Press, 1963). The unrivaled introduction to the concept of the orders.

14. A thorough survey of the development of the classical orders emphasizing the aspect of meaning from antiquity through the Renaissance is being prepared by the art historian John Onians. The book will be published by Princeton University Press.

15. Guarino Guarini, *Architettura Civile,* facsimile of the 1737 edition (London: Gregg Press, 1964).

CHAPTER 1

1. Vitruvius (Morgan) p. 5.

2. Gerd Neumann, "Verwehtes Kapitell," *Jahrbuch fur 1981-82, Deutsches Archiketurmuseum* (Wiesbaden: Friedr. Vieweg & Sohn, 1981), pp. 182-83. The translation is by Tim Steele.

3. Barry Bergdoll, "Prototypes and Archetypes: Deutsches Archiketurmuseum, Frankfurt, West Germany," *Architectural Record* (New York: McGraw Hill, August 1984), pp. 104-17.

4. Marina Bonavia, Rosamaria Francucci, and Rosa Mezzina, "San Carlo alle Quattro Fontane: le fasi della costruzione," *La Nuova Italia Scientifica, Ricerche di Storia dell'Architettura Barocca* (Rome, 1983), pp. 39-65. Joseph Connors kindly brought this publication to my attention. The speculations on Borromini's iconographic intent in the design of the capitals is based on conversations with Joseph Connors and John Beldon Scott. See also:

Leo Steinberg, *Borromini's San Carlo alle Quattro Fontane: A Study in Multiple Form and Architectural Symbolism,* Revised Garland edition of a dissertation of 1960 (New York, 1977).

5. Vitruvius's passage on the importance of history for the architect is one of the early statements of his treatise. It is found in his wonderful chapter, "The Education of the Architect," bk. I, chap. I (Morgan) pp. 1-17.

6. Vitruvius, *On Architecture,* bk. IV, chap. II, 2, trans. Frank Granger (1932) (Cambridge: Harvard University Press, 1962).

7. Franco Borsi, *Il Disegno interrotto: Tratatti Medicci d'Architetturae* (Florence: Edizione Gonnellio, 1980). Publication of ms. by Gherardo Spini, "I Tre Primi Libri Sopra l'Instritzioni de' Greci et Latini Architettori," in *Tratatti inèditi,* Biblioteca Nazionale Marciana di Venezia, Ms. It. IV 38 (5543).

8. William Chambers, *A Treatise on the Decorative Part of Civil Architecture,* (1791), facsimile (New York: Benjamin Blom, Inc., 1963), p. 17. For other views on the origin of the Doric order see:

Joseph Rykwerk, *On Adam's House in Paradise* (New York: Museum of Modern Art, 1972).

Quinlan Terry, "The Origins of the Classical Orders," *Archives d'Architecture Moderne,* no. 26 (Bruxelles, 1984): pp. 35-49.

John Wood, *The Origin of Building: (Or, The Plagiarism of the Heathens Detected),* (Bath, 1741), facsimile (Farnborough, England: Gregg International, 1968).

Quinlan Terry's construction of Chamber's "third sort of hut" as a garden pavilion built between 1976 and 1980 at West Green, an estate in England, provides little development beyond this eighteenth-century source. The limitations of this approach are more glaring in Terry's article written to explain the origin of the orders. He proposes the idea that the perfection of the orders presupposes their ordination to the Jews by Divine intervention. Terry neither gives credit to John Wood the Elder as the source of this bizarre theory nor is he open to the resources of the present which can increase our understanding of classical architecture.

9. A. Von Gerkan, "Die Herkunft des Dorischen Gebälks," *Jahrbuch des Deutshcen Archäologischen Instituts (Berlin: Walter de Gruyter & Co., 1948), pp. 1-13.*

10. The various publications of the Temple of Apollo at Thermon have not presented it in clear graphic terms. To my knowledge, only one full reconstruction has been accomplished, an eccentric realization by Immo Beyer, "Der Triglyphenfries von Thermos C, Ein Kostruktionvorschlag," Deutsches Archaologisches Institut Jahrbuch (1972), pp. 197-226. The most helpful references in English are:

J. Charbonneaux, *Archaic Greek Art* (London: Thames and Hudson, 1971), p. 32.

R. M. Cook, "The Archetypal Doric Temple," *Annual of the British School at Athens* no. 65 (1970): pp. 17-19.

Coulton, *Ancient Greek Architects at Work,* pp. 35-43.

Georgios Soteriades, "The Greek Excavations at Thermos," *Records of the Past* vol. 1 (January 1902): pp. 172-81.

The primary archaeological publications are:

Georgios Soteriades, "Thermos," *Ephemeris Archaeologia* (Athens, 1900), pp. 162-211.

Georgios Soteriades, "Der Apollotempel zu Thermos," *Antike Denkmaeler* (Berlin: Georg Reimer, 1908).

I owe many thanks to classicists Margaret Miles and Gretchen Umholtz for help they have provided in my reconstruction of the Temple of Apollo at Thermon. Umholtz translated numerous articles from Greek and German and provided valuable analysis in a class she taught on the prototypical Doric order for the San Francisco Architectural Club in spring 1986.

For the perspective in figure 1.11 I have employed the reconstruction of the entablature published by Soteriades in *Antike Denkmaeler.* I recognize that there are inconsistencies in its detail, but have postponed attempting to resolve them until I can study the site and the artifacts firsthand. Many of these questions of detail, as well as larger issues, may never be answered. Did the architrave have guttae? What did the columns look like and what was the form of the roof? The persistence of terra cotta and the decay of the wooden structure force one to draw these forms mirroring the earliest surviving stone structures. We may be doomed to incorrectness, but we can only test the possible appearance of Thermon by making the hypothesis graphic and specific.

11. Ovid, "Prokne and Philomela," in *The Metamorphosis,* trans. Rolfe Humphries (Bloomington: Indiana University Press, 1955). Many versions of the story exist and the name Philomela is almost exclusively found instead of Chelidon. An abstract of the myth is presented in Roland Howe and Erika Simon, *The Birth of Greek Art* (New York: Oxford University Press, 1981), p. 105:

". . . King Pandion had two daughters, Prokne and Philomela. Prokne was married to Tereus of Thrace and had by him a son, Itys. She made her husband travel to Athens and bring back her sister. Tereus fell in love with Philomela, raped her and cut out her tongue so that she could not betray him. But somehow Philomela made the crime known to her sister. Prokne and Philomela therefore killed the son, Itys, and offered him as a dish to Tereus at a sacrificial feast. When Tereus discovered what he had eaten, he pursued his wife, his sword drawn. Zeus, however, changed him into a hoopoe, his wife into a nightingale (Aedon), who for ever after wept for her son Itys, and Philomela into a swallow (Chelidon)."

12. Howe, Thomas Noble, *The Invention of the Doric Order* (diss., Harvard University, Ann Arbor: University Microfilms, 1985, text-fiche). This work reviews the history of attempts to answer the question of the origin of the Doric, and it analyzes the theoretical motives that underlie the various points of view. Although the archaeological evidence is reviewed, new reconstructions are not attempted. A strong argument is presented for the spontaneous development of the Doric order by combining various foreign models with native traditions, possibly at the hands of a single individual.

13. In figures 1.12 to 1.22, I illustrate the principles of hierarchy and order that are conveyed by the method of articulating the form and materials of the classical elements in a number of Roman Baroque buildings. An

early version of these observations was published in a German translation as: Thomas Gordon Smith, "Die Gabe des Janus," *Jahrbuch fur Architektur 1983, Deutsches Architekturmuseum* (Wiesbaden: Friedr. Vieweg & Sohn, 1983), pp. 145-50.

I was first sparked to study the development of formal themes of successive generations of Roman Baroque architects by the photographic comparisons of the Palazzo dei Conservatori and Sant' Andrea al Quirinale in Summerson's *The Classical Language of Architecture* (Cambridge: MIT Press, 1963). A graphic analysis of the origins of these systems in Renaissance practice is presented in: Paolo Portoghesi, "The Language of Roman Classicism," *Rome of the Renaissance, trans.* Pearl Sanders (New York: Phaidon, 1972), pp. 353-64.

A general guide to the buildings cited and specific books or articles that analyze the articulation of these buildings follow:

General
Anthony Blunt, *Guide to Baroque Rome* (New York: Harper and Row, 1982).

Paolo Portoghesi, *Roma Barocca: The History of an Architectonic Culture,* trans. Barbara Luigia La Penta (Cambridge: MIT Press, 1970).

Rudolf Wittkower, *Art and Architecture in Italy 1600-1750* (Harmondsworth, England: Penguin Books, 1978).

Michelangelo

James S. Ackerman, *The Architecture of Michelangelo,* 2nd ed. (Chicago: University of Chicago Press, 1986).

Elizabeth MacDougall, "Michelangelo and the Porta Pia," *Journal of the Society of Architectural Historians* (1960), pp. 97-108.

Paolo Portoghesi and Bruno Zevi, *Michelangiolo Architetto* (Torino: Giulio Einaudi editore, 1964).

Maderno

Howard Hibbard, *Carolo Maderno and Roman Architecture 1580-1630* (London: A. Zwemmer, 1972).

Borromini

Anthony Blunt, *Borromini* (Cambridge: Harvard University Press, 1979).

Joseph Connors, *Borromini and the Roman Oratory, Style, and Society* (New York: Architectural History Foundation, 1980).

Paolo Portoghesi, *Borromini: Architettura come Linguaggio* (Rome: Electa Edizioni, 1967).

Paolo Portoghesi, *Borromini nella cultura europea* (Rome: Officina, 1964).

Bernini

Franco Borsi, *Bernini,* trans. Robert Erich Wolf (New York: Rizzoli, 1984).

Franco Borsi, *La Chiesa di S. Andrea al Quirinale* (Rome: Officina Edizione, 1967).

Joseph Connors, "Bernini's S. Andrea al Quirinale: Payments and Planning," *Journal of the Society of Architectural Historians* 41 (1982): pp. 15-37.

T. K. Kitao, "Bernini's Church Facades: Methods of Design and the Contrapposti," *Journal of the Society of Architectural Historians* 24 (1965): pp. 263-84.

Richard Krautheimer, *The Rome of Alexander VII: 1655-1667* (Princeton: Princeton University Press, 1985), p. 62. Krautheimer asserts that the convex Ionic entablature that forms the porch of Sant' Andrea was not an original feature, ". . . the convex colonnaded porch was added by Bernini only after 1670." Originally, the building had only three concentric steps to the portico.

14. T. Ashby, "Sixteenth Century Drawings of Roman Buildings Attributed to Andreas Coner," *Papers of the British School at Rome* (London: MacMillan & Co., 1904).

This reduced reproduction of the Coner manuscript is a valuable reference for ancient moulding profiles.

15. Portoghesi and Zevi, *Michelangiolo Architetto.* Examples of additional drawings made from the Coner manuscript are reproduced in this volume.

16. H. Thelen, *Francesco Borromini: Die Handzeichnungen* (Graz, Austria: Akademische Druck und Verlagsanstalt, 1967). Examples of additional Borromini drawings made from the Coner manuscript are reproduced in this volume. Figure 1-24 is reproduced from the Ashby text. Ashby notes that the "Porta Scura" is beneath a portico in Tivoli connected with the Temple of Hercules.

17. The most readily available editions of Vitruvius, Palladio, and Chambers were cited in note 11 of the Introduction. An overall survey of the tradition of treatises since the Renaissance is:

Dora Wiebenson, *Architectural Theory and Practice from Alberti to Ledoux* (Chicago: University of Chicago Press, Architectural Publications, Inc., 1982).

Editions of the other treatises cited follow:

Leone Battista Alberti, *Ten Books on Architecture,* trans. James Leoni (1726), ed. Joseph Rykwert (London: Alec Tiranti, 1965) and (New York: Dover, 1986).
Rykwert is completing a new translation and analysis of Alberti for the Architectural History Foundation. This reprint of the Leoni translation is currently the most accessible publication in English. An Italian translation from the original Latin is available in:

Leon Battista Alberti, *L'Architettura, (De Re Aedificatoria),* trans. Giovanni Orlandi (Milano: Edizioni il Polifilo, 1966).

Marc-Antoine Laugier, *An Essay on Architecture,* trans. Wolfgang and Anni Herrmann (Los Angeles: Hennessey & Ingalls, Inc., 1977).

Claude Perrault, *Ordonnance des Cinq Èspeces de Colonnes Selon la Mèthode des Anciens* (Paris: J. B. Coignard, 1683).

Claude Perrault, *A Treatise on the Five Orders of Architecture,* trans. of *Ordonnance des Cinq Èspeces* by John James (London, 1722).

The influential *Regola delli cinque ordini d'architettura* of Giacomo Barozzi da Vignola has been excluded from this list because it is limited to the function of a canon. Reprints of the original edition of 1562 are scarce. Massively-revised versions have employed the name but often alter Vignola's intent. The *Vignola* of Pierre Esquie, published through the 1930s, and the handy *Le Vignole du Poche* of 1896 by E. J. Thierry must be seen as nineteenth-century French publications. *The American Vignola,* a heavy-handed reference by William R. Ware, has unfortunately gained acceptance as being authoritative due to its recent republication in the Classical America Series.

18. Vitruvius, Musical harmony and its application to architectural proportion, bk. V, chap. IV-V; bk. X, chap. II-X; bk. VII, chap. I-XIV. Weather and national temperament, bk. VI, chap. I.

19. Carol Herselle Krinsky, "Seventy-Eight Vitruvius Manuscripts," *Journal of the Warburg and Courtauld Institutes* vol. 30 (London: University of London, 1967): pp. 36-70. This study provides an excellent catalogue of the surviving manuscripts.

20. Heinrich Klotz and John Onians have kindly shared their views on the Carolingian contribution to the Vitruvian tradition.

21. Vitruvius, bk. VII, Introduction, pp. 12-15. The influence of Vitruvius on subsequent authors:

William Hugh Plommer, *Vitruvius and Later Roman Building Manuals* (Cambridge: The University Press, 1973).

For brief discussions of the ancient tradition of writing treatises:

J. J. Pollitt, *The Ancient View of Greek Art: Criticism, History and Terminology* (New Haven: Yale University Press, 1974), pp. 12-13.

F. W. Schlikker, *Hellenistische Vorstellungen von der Schönheir des Bauwerks nach Vitruv* (Berlin, 1940).

22. Ekrem Akurgal, *Ancient Civilizations and Ruins of Turkey* (Istanbul: Haset Kitabevi, 1985), pp. 139-42, 177-206.

Otto Bauer, "Des Athena-Tempels zu Priene," *Mitteilungen des deutschen archäologischen Instituts. Abteilung Istanbul* 18 (1968): pp. 212-20.

H. Drerup, *Zum Artemistempel von Magnesia* (Marburg, W. Germany: Marburger Winckelmann Programm, 1964), pp. 13-22.

Carl Humann, *Magnesia am Maeander* (Berlin: G. Reimer, 1904).

A. W. Lawrence, rev. R. A. Tomlinson, *Greek Architecture* (New York: Penguin Books, 1983), pp. 250, 282-83.

Society of Dilettanti, *Antiquities of Ionia* vol. 4 (London, 1881).

23. Vitruvius, *The Ten Books on Architecture,* bk VII, Introduction, trans. Morris Hicky Morgan (1914) (New York: Dover Publications, Inc., 1960), pp. 12-15.

24. Erik Forssman, *Dorisch, Jonisch, Korinthish, Studien über den Gebrauch der Säulenordnungen in der Architektur des 16-18 Jahrhunderts* (Stockholm: Almquist & Wiksell, 1961, Wiesbaden: Friedr. Vieweg & Sohn, 1983). I owe many thanks to Georg Rattay for making a rough translation of this book into English. The notion of Bramante's fuller comprehension of Vitruvius is presented, and the associations of character with the orders is approached not only from the well-known Italian examples but also in relation to the interpretation of the Northern European Renaissance.

25. Palladio, *I Quattro Libri,* bk. I, chap. XIV-XV.

26. James S. Ackerman, *Palladio* (Baltimore: Penguin Books, 1967), p. 27.

Barbaro, Danielle, *I Dieci libri dell' architettura di Vitruvio Pollione tradutti et commentati da Monsignor Barbaro Patriarca di Aguileggia* (Venice, 1556), *Manoscritti preparatori,* Bibliotecca Marciana, Cod.H. IV, 152, (5106) and 35 (5133). The importance of Palladio's graphic and architectural interpretation for this translation is apparent after looking at Barbaro's preparatory manuscript. The few crudely sketched illustrations, presumably in Barbaro's hand, show no innate understanding of the proportional requirements of Vitruvian architecture. Ackerman suggests Palladio's active role in interpreting the translation into architectonic terms.

27. Claude Perrault, *Les Dix Livres d'Architecture de Vitruve* (Paris, 1673). Facsimile by Pierre Mardaga, ed. (Bruxelles, 1979). Two other editions of Vitruvius are well illustrated and interesting for architects:

Della Architettura di Gio. Antonio Rusconi . . . Secondo precetti di Vitruvio . . . (Venice, 1590).

Vitruve, ed. Choisy (Paris, 1909). Reprinted (Paris: F. de Nobele, 1971).

28. Wolfgang Hermann, *The Theory of Claude Perrault* (London: A. Zwemmer, 1973), pp. 95-129.

29. William Chambers, *Civil Architecture* (1791), p. 19. "Indeed none of the few things now existing in Greece, though so pompously described, and neatly represented, in various publications of our time, seem to deserve great notice . . . nor do they seem calculated to throw new light upon the art, or to contribute to its advancement. . . ."

James Stuart and Nicholas Revett, *The Antiquities of Athens* vols. 1, 2, 3 (London, 1762), p. i. Facsimile (New York: Benjamin Blom, Inc., 1968).

" . . . as Greece was the great Mistress of the Arts, and Rome, in this respect, no more than her disciple, it may be presumed, all the most admired buildings which adorned that imperial city, were but imitations of Grecian Originals."

Eileen Harris, "Rome and Greece" in "Comments on *The Treatise on Civil Architecture*" in John Harris, *Sir William Chambers, Knight of the Polish Star* (University Park: Pennsylvania State University Press, 1970).

30. My observations of the prevalence of Venetian Gothic holdovers in the architecture of early sixteenth-century Vicenza relate to Palladio. For the general conflict:

Rudolph Wittkower, *Gothic vs. Classic: Architectural Projects in Seventeenth Century Italy,* ed. Margot Wittkower (New York: Braziller, 1974).

31. Philo's Arsenal has been the subject of numerous books and reconstructions completed almost entirely by Scandinavians. English translations of the specifications are reproduced in the works by Bundgaard and Jeppesen. My students have found Jerome J. Pollitt's translation to be particularly useful in their reconstruction projects.

J. A. Bundgaard, *Mnesicles, A Greek Architect at Work* (Gyldendal: Scandinavian University Books, 1957), pp. 117-32. A translation of the inscription and analysis form a portion of this book.

Auguste Choisy, *L'Arsenal du Pirèe* (Paris: Librairie de la Societe Anonyme de Publications Periodiques, 1883), pp. 31-37 and pls. 1 and 2. A geometric proportional scheme and precise engraved plates distinguish this early attempt to reconstruct the inscription.

Coulton, *Ancient Greek Architects at Work.* See pp. 54-55 for a general discussion of Philo's Arsenal and the light that this inscription sheds on Greek architectural practice.

Kristian Jeppesen, *Paradeigmata: Three Mid-fourth Century Main Works of Hellenic Architecture Reconsidered* (Denmark: Aarhus University Press, Jutland Archaeological Society Publications, vol. 4, 1958). This book provides a translation, a minute commentary on the meaning of structural terms, and a restoration of the Arsenal.

Eivind Lorenzen, *The Arsenal at Piraeus* (Copenhagen: Gads Forlag, 1964). This author presents a bizarre contradiction of previous interpretations.

Vilhelm Marstrand, *Arsenalet i Piraeus og Oldtidens Byggeregler* (Copenhagen: Egmont H. Petersens, 1922). This is a beautifully illustrated book that contains comparisons of previous reconstructions as well as a full bibliography of publications that include the early reconstructions of Fabricius (1882) and Dörpfeld (1883).

Jerome J. Politt, *The Art of Greece, 1400-31 B.C.* (Englewood Cliffs, N.J.: Prentice-Hall,

Inc., 1965), pp. 185-88.

In a review of reconstructions of Philo's Arsenal by students at Yale in 1986, Professor Politt pointed out that the specification was intended to provide a general standard for the citizens who were appointed public overseers to evaluate the quality of the building's construction. The exact dimensions may be a simplification of the components. This helps to resolve a number of inconsistencies that arrive when one attempts to reconstruct the building.

32. F. Courby, "Temple des Atheniens" in *Dèlos: Ecole Françcaise d'Athènes* (Paris: E. De Boccard, 1931). This reconstruction of the Athenian Temple to Apollo on Delos shows its many similarities to the Parthenon. The configuration of the sculptural acroteria has been reassessed in:

Antoine Hermary, "La Sculpture Archaïque et Classique, I" in *Exploration Archèologique de Dèlos* (Paris: Diffusion de Boccard, 1984).

33. Vitruvius, *Ten Books*, bk. VII, 13, Morgan trans., p. 198.

Richard Sittwell, "Peiraeus" in *The Princeton Encyclopedia of Classical Sites* (Princeton: Princeton University Press, 1976), p. 107.

"In 86 B.C. the Athenians revolted to obtain their freedom, but the conquest of the city by Sulla was the result. The walls of the city and of Peiraeus were demolished by the victorious Roman General who sought in this way the diminution of Athens' power."

34. Arnaldo Bruschi, *Bramante* (London: Thames and Hudson, 1977), p. 87. Bruschi notes that the Spanish Cardinal Carvaja was in charge of the Tempietto in 1502. Although the exact date of the Tempietto design is unknown, Bruschi cites 1502 as the year the Spanish crown decided to build on the supposed site of St. Peter's crucifixion. See also:

Arnaldo Bruschi, *Bramante, Architetto* (Bari, Italy: Editori Laterza, 1969), pp. 463-527.

35. Bruschi, *Bramante,* pp. 30-32. "Peter was a hero of Christianity—a kind of Christian Hercules . . . the Doric order was the obvious logical choice." This argument is presented less stridently in:

Earl Rosenthal, "The Antecedents of Bramante's Tempietto," *Journal of the Society of Architectural Historians* (May 1964), pp. 55-74. "Certainly the Doric Order was more appropriate for a monument dedicated to the venerable Saint Peter."

36. Bruschi and Rosenthal analyze numerous factors that may have influenced Bramante in the design of the Tempietto, but neither have noted the mundane problem of working with salvaged columns as a factor in resolving its proportional balance. I do not know the provenance of the monolithic column shafts, but their battered mouldings and the difference in material between the shafts, capitals and bases suggests that they are ancient turnings.

In the note "to the reader" in the fourth of his *The Five Books of Architecture,* Sebastiano Serlio comments, ". . . and how we should helpe ourselves with pieces of other buildings, with such things as are to be used, and at other times have stood in worke."

In 1979 Christian Norberg Schulz made me aware of the prevalence during the Renaissance and Baroque periods of employing architectural salvage, *spolia.* In addition to economy, the lack of stone such as granite or marble in the area of Rome, and perhaps the totemic reasons for incorporating ancient workmanship into a new construction, were factors that lead to the practice of reusing parts of ancient buildings. The destruction of ancient monuments during the Renaissance for this and other purposes is recounted in:

Roberto Weiss, *The Renaissance Discovery of Classical Antiquity (Oxford: B. Blackwell, 1969).*

37. J. D. Beazley, "The Excavations at Al Mina, Sueidia, III. The Red-Figured Vases," The Journal of Hellenic Studies (London, 1939), pp. 36-38. "The use of the bucrane in fourth century vases may point to a similar use in contemporary architecture, but this is not certain. What is certain is that both uses were derived from the practice of decorating sanctuaries and other buildings with the actual skulls of slaughtered animals, alternating with other real objects."

See also:

W. B. Dinsmoor, "Bucrania," *American Journal of Archaeology* (1910). p. 178.

Antonio Giuliano, *Museo Nazionale Romano, Le Sculture* vol. 1, no. 7 (Rome: De Luca Editore, 1980): p. 469.

38. The Metropolitan Museum of Art, New York. The label of the boukranion in figure 1.33 notes that, "Painted skulls of oxen, goats . . . placed in graves and nonfunerary deposits in Sudan-Mid Egypt . . . a foreign burial practice to Egypt and the presence of weapons suggests that they may be the graves of mercenaries."

39. Jeppesen, *Paradeigmata,* p. 69, notes: "The architect Philo of Eleusis submitted his plans . . . and in an eloquent and persuasive speech he succeeded in stirring the enthusiasm of the Athenians whose patriotism was challenged at that time by the menace from Macedonia. . . ."

40. Joseph Connors, *Borromini and the Roman Oratory, Style and Society* (New York: Architectural History Foundation, 1980), pp. 23-28, 96-100.

Connors' review of M. Heimburger Ravalli, *Archiettetura scultura e arti minori nel barocco italiano. Ricerche nell' Archivio Spada* (Florence, 1977), and of L. Neppi, *Palazzo Spada* (Rome, 1975), in *Journal of the Society of Architectural Historians* 38 (1979): pp. 193-96.

41. Francesco Borromini and Virgilio Spada, *Opus architectonicum Equitis Francisci Borromini* (Rome, 1725), facsimile (Farnborough, England: Gregg International, 1963).

42. Connors, *Borromini and the Roman Oratory,* p. 38. The photograph of Borromini's drawing of the Pamphilj Pantheon scheme is a detail of drawing no. 285 in the Albertina Collection in Vienna.

CHAPTER 2

1. Oscar Edwards, stanza from poem quoted, but not cited, in William Charles Hays, *Order, Taste and Grace in Architecture* (Berkeley: University of California Regional Oral History Program, 1961), p. 122.

2. Axel Boethius and J. B. Ward-Perkins, *Etruscan and Roman Architecture* (Harmondsworth: The Pelican History of Art, 1970), pp. 37-64, 130-33. Boethius criticizes Vitruvius's reduction of the variety of Etruscan architectural forms into a canonical Tuscan type, but gives Vitruvius no credit for having preserved the concept of the Tuscan order in bk. IV, chap. VII.

Frank E. Brown, *Cosa, the Making of a Roman Town* (Ann Arbor: University of Michigan Press, 1980).

3. James S. Ackerman, "The Tuscan/Rustic Order: A Study in the Metaphorical Language of Architecture," *Journal of the Society of Architectural Historians* 42 (March 1983): pp. 15-34.

4. Sources employed to devise the proportions of the Doric order are:

Francis Cranmer Penrose, *An Investigation of the Principles of Athenian Architecture* (London: The Society of Dilettanti, Macmillan and Co., 1888).

Vitruvius, *The Ten Books on Architecture,* bk. IV, chap. III.

5. Determining a canonical color scheme for the Doric order is difficult due to conflicting archaeological opinions and a certain variety that existed in antiquity. The most helpful resources are:

Ècole des Beaux-Arts, *Paris, Rome, Athens, Le Voyage en Grèce des Architectes Francaise aux XIXe et XXe Siecles* (Paris, 1982), 162-71.

L. Fenger, *Die Dorische Polychromie* (Berlin, 1886).

Leon Victor Solon, *Polychromy, Architectural and Structural: Theory and Practice* (New York: The Architectural Record, 1924).

The interest in classical polychromy at the Ecole des Beaux-Arts in the second half of the nineteenth century became inventive rather than archaeological. An extreme example is the well-published reconstruction of the Parthenon by Benoit Loviot that makes more of a comment on Neo-Grec taste than the sensibility of Iktinos and Kallikrates. This development, however natural for creative architects, confused perception of ancient practice. For a view of the interest and controversy that polychromy generated in France, see:

Arthur Drexler, *The Architecture of the Ecole des Beax Arts* (Cambridge: Museum of Modern Art/MIT Press, 1977).

David Van Zanten, *The Architectural Polychromy of the 1830's* (New York: Garland Publishing, Inc., 1977).

6. Vitruvius, *The Ten Books of Architecture,* bk. IV, chap. III, 1-10, Morgan trans., pp. 109-110.

7. The development of the Ionic order has inspired less speculation and study than the Doric. Vitruvius is matter-of-fact in terms of its origins in bk. IV, chap. I and its technique in bk. III, chap. V. Several studies that survey its development in Asia Minor are:

Ekrem Akurgal, "The Early Period and Golden Age of Ionia," *American Journal of Archaeology,* Archaeological Institute of America (October 1962), pp. 369-79.

Anton Bammer, *Die Architektur des Jüngeren Artemision von Ephesos* (Wiesbaden: Franz Steiner, 1972).

John Boardman, "Chian and Early Ionic Architecture," *The Antiquaries Journal* (Oxford University Press, July-October 1959), pp. 170-218.

Otto Puchstein, "Das Ionische Capitell," *Winckelmannsfeste der Archaeologischen Gesellschaft zu Berlin* (Berlin: Georg Reimer, 1887).

Oskar Reuther, *Der Heratempel von Samos, der Bau Seit der Zeit Des Polykrates* (Berlin: Gebr. Mann, 1957).

8. J. T. Wood, *The Discoveries of Ephesos* (London, 1877).

9. Howard Crosby Butler, *Sardis, Publication of the American Society for the Excavation of Sardis* vol. 2, part 1. "The Temple of Artemis" (Leyden: Late E. Brill, Ltd., 1925) pp. 65-72.

10. C. R. Cockerell, *The Temples of Jupiter Panhellenius at Aegina and of Apollo Epicurius at Bassae* (London, 1860).

William Bell Dinsmoor, "The Temple of Apollo at Bassae," *Metropolitan Museum Studies* (1933), pp. 204-227.

Vincent Scully, *The Earth, the Temple, and the Gods: Greek Sacred Architecture* (New Haven: Yale University Press, 1962). Scully's passion for the Temple of Apollo at Bassae inspired Frederick Cooper of the University of Minnesota to conduct a thorough study of the building which will be published in a monograph.

11. Philip P. Betancourt, *The Aeolic Style in Architecture: A Survey of Its Development in Palestine, the Halikarnassos Peninsula and Greece, 1000-500 B.C.* (Princeton: Princeton University Press, 1977).

12. The simple Samian base had little influence. The Ephesian base, however, became canonical in Asia Minor. Vitruvius describes the type in bk. III, chap. V, 3, as an alternative to the Attic base. Although the Ephesian base had no influence on Roman architecture, Vitruvius's description must have been read attentively by Carlo Maderno about 1600. He employed the form for the Ionic columns on the facade of St. Peters at the Vatican.

Coulton, *Ancient Greek Architects at Work*, pp. 100-102. Discussion of the evolution of the Ionic base.

An ancient resource for constructing the profile of the Ephesian base and methods for establishing the entasis of a column shaft has been discovered at the Temple of Apollo at Didyma. Articles which present this research are:

Lothar Haselberger, "The Construction Plans for the Temple of Apollo at Didyma," *Scientific American* vol. 253, no. 6 (December 1985): pp. 126-32.

"Werkzeichnungen am Jüngeren Didymeion Vorbericht," *Istanbuler Mitteilungen Deutschen Archäologischen Instituts,Abteilung Istanbul* Band 30 (Tübingen, W. Germany: Ernst Wasmuth, 1980): pp. 191-215.

Two sources that treat moldings and refinements in the orders are:

Lucy T. Shoe, *Profiles of Greek Mouldings* (Cambridge: Harvard University Press, 1936).

Gorham Philip Stevens, "Entasis of Roman Columns," *Memoirs of the American Academy in Rome* 4 (New York, 1924): pp. 121-52.

13. Heinrich Bauer, *Korinthische Kapitelle Des 4. und 3. Jahrhunderts v. Chr.* (Berlin: Gebr. Mann Verlag, 1973).

14. Georges Roux, *L'Architecture de L'Argolide aux IVe et IIIe Siecles avant J.-C.* (Paris: Editions de Boccard, 1961), pp. 171-200.

15. D. S. Robertson, *Greek and Roman Architecture* (Cambridge: The University Press, 1969), p. 204.

Burkhardt Wesenberg, *Beitage zur Rekonstrucktion Griechischer Architektur nach Literarischen Quellen* (Berlin: Gebr. Mann Verlag, 1983), p. 20. The construction of the Corinthian/Doric tetrastyle in Wesenberg is probably closer to what Vitruvius had in mind than the provincial "Corinthian/Doric" temple at Paestum.

16. I have relied on the Pantheon and Renaissance sources for construction of the Corinthian entablature.

17. D. E. Strong, "Some Early Examples of the Composite Capital," *Journal of Roman Studies* (London, 1960), pp. 119-28.

18. Andrea Pozzo, *Rules and Examples of Perspective, Proper for Painters and Architects (1693),* trans. John James, 1707, facsimile (New York: Benjamin Blom, Inc., 1971,) figure LIIB.

Methods for constructing the Solomonic column shaft have been demonstrated by Vignola and Guarini (see figure 1.28). The clearest method, however, is presented by

Pozzo, the painter of the remarkable *Tromp-d'oeil* ceiling in the Church of Sant' Ignazio in Rome.

Renaissance and Baroque architects associated the Roman serpentine column shafts at St. Peters with the Temple of Solomon due to their rich ornamentation. Numerous examples of Solomonic columns will be presented in the forthcoming:

Stanley Tigerman, *The Architecture of Exile* (New York: Rizzoli, 1988).

CHAPTER 3

1. Joseph Connors, *Borromini and the Roman Oratory, Style and Society* (New York: Architectural History Foundation, 1980), p. 75. The passage is translated from Borromini's *Opus Architectonicum*, 3r, xix, 53r, written with Virgilio Spada in 1647.

2. Paolo Portoghesi, *Roma Barocca, the History of an Architectonic Culture* (Cambridge: MIT Press, 1970), pp. 51-52, 536. The diatribe against the Mannerist approach to invention was cited to Portoghesi by Diana Risioli from a manuscript by Pirro Ligorio dated from about 1550.

David Summers, *Michelangelo and the Language of Art* (Princeton: Princeton University Press, 1981), pp. 269-300. Summers interprets the work and thought of Michelangelo in the light of rule and invention in his essays, "Paragone," "Imitation," and "Ordine."

3. The following books focus on some of the noncolumnar aspects of Greek architecture:

W. B. Dinsmore, Jr., *Ancient Athenian Building Methods* (Athens: American School of Classical Studies, 1984, dist. by Princeton University Press).

Alfred Hodge, *The Woodwork of Greek Roofs* (Cambridge: Cambridge University Press, 1960).

Robert Lorentz Scranton, *Greek Walls* (Cambridge: Harvard University Press, 1941).

4. Christian C. F. Heulsen, "Das Septizonium des Septimius Severus," *Sechsundvierzigstes Programm zum Winckelmannsfeste der Archaeologischen Gesellschaft zu Berlin (Berlin, 1886), pp. 2-36.*

Sebastiano Serlio, The Five Books of Architecture, 1611, bk. III, chap. IV, fol. 36, facsimile (New York: Dover Publications, Inc., 1982).

Enrico Stevenson, "Il Settizonio severiano e la distruzione dei suoi avanzi sotto Sisto V," *Bulletino della Commissione Archeologica di Roma* (1887-88), pp. 269-98.

The Septizonium was built in Rome in 203 A.D. It consisted of three tiers of Corinthian porticoes and was demolished in the late sixteenth century.

5. Dora Wiebenson, *Sources of Greek Revival Architecture* (London: A. Zwemmer, 1969), p. 127.

6. John Ruskin, *The Stones of Venice,* vol. 3, "The Fall," chap. IV, XXXV (New York: E.P. Dutton and Co., Inc., 1927), p. 177.

7. J. J. Coulton, *Ancient Greek Architects at Work* (Ithaca: Cornell University Press, 1977), pp. 55, 72.

8. James S. Ackerman, *Palladio* (Baltimore: Penguin, 1966), pp. 26-27, 34.

9. Vitruvius, *The Ten Books on Architecture,* bk. IV, chap. III, 3, trans. Morris Hicky Morgan (1914) (New York: Dover Publications, Inc., 1960) p. 110.

10. Paul Schazmann, "Das Gymnasion, der Tempelbezirk der Hera Basileia," *Altertümer von Pergamon,* vol. VI & Tafeln (Berlin: Walter de Gruyter & Co., 1923), pp. 102-110, pls. XVIII, XXXII-XXXV.

11. Ottavio Bertotti Scamozzi, *Le Fabbriche e i Disegni di Andrea Palladio* (Vicenza, 1796), pls. IX-XII.

12. Paola Zancani Montuoro and U. Zanotti-Bianco, *Heraion alla Foce del Sele* (Rome: La Libreria dello Stato, 1951), pls. XXXIX-LIX.

13. P. E. Hoff and M. L. Stephensen, "Le Tresor des Atheniens," *Fouilles de Delphes* (Paris: E. de Boccard, 1933).

14. Fernand Courby, "Les Temples d'Apollon," *Dèlos,* Fascicule XII (Paris: E. de Boccard, 1931).

Antoine Hermary, "La Sculpture Archaïque et Classique," *Dèlos,* Fascicule XXXIV (Paris: Diffusion de Boccard, 1984).

15. Richard Delbrueck, *Hellenistische Bauten in Latium* (Strassburg: Karl J. Trübner, 1907), pp. 24-36.

16. Minna Heimburger-Rivalli, "Disegni Sconosciuti del Borromini Per il Banco di Santo Spirito e Per Palazzo Spada," *Paragone Arte* vol. 275 (1973): pp. 57-63.

Richard Krautheimer, *The Rome of Alexander VII, 1655-1667,* p. 46. Krautheimer comments that Borromini submitted three versions of this facade to Alexander VII before he accepted, "the most reticent and 'classical' ever designed by Borromini."

17. Paolo Portoghesi, *The Rome of Borromini: Architecture as Language,* trans. Barbara Luigia La Penta (New York: George Braziller, 1967), pp. 281-90, pls. 157-63.

18. Cesere D'Onofrio, *Roma nel Seicento* (Florence: Vallecchi, 1968), pp. 199-201. First publication of a manuscript by Fioravante Martinelli written about 1660 entitled, *Roma ornata dall' architettura, pittura e scultura.* A translation of the description of the Palazzo della Propaganda Fide reads, ". . . the Doric column made according to the ancients without a base, as Andrea Palladio demonstrated in his Book on Architecture . . . and as we see at the Palazzo Savelli which was once the Theater of Marcellus. . . ." Joseph Connors speculates that this comment quotes Borromini's defense in response to criticism from Bernini, whose apartments were across the street on eye level with the baseless columns of the window surrounds.

19. Christian Norberg Schulz, *Kilian Ignaz Dientzenhofer e il Barocco Boemo* (Rome: Officina Edizione, 1968), pp. 81-83.

20. American School of Correspondence, *Cyclopedia of Architecture, Carpentry and Building* (Chicago, 1907), pp. 203-204.

21. Gilles-Marie Oppenort, drawing of a Doric entablature in "Album of Architectural Drawings," Ms. Cooper Hewitt Collection, New York. Joseph Connors first showed me this sketchbook which is one of several that survive from Oppenort's stay in Rome between 1692 and 1699. Elaine Dee of the Cooper-Hewitt has kindly provided much information about Oppenort and his sketchbooks.

22. Caroline Constant, *The Palladio Guide* (Princeton: Princeton Architectural Press, 1985), pp. 71-72.

Giuseppe Mazzotti, *Ville Venete* (Rome: C. Bestetti, 1963).

23. Vitruvius, *The Ten Books,* bk. III, chap. III, 8, Morgan trans., pp. 82-84. "These rules for symmetry were established by Hermogenes, who was the first to devise the principle of the pseudo dipteral octastyle. . . . Hermogenes produced results which exhibit much acute ingenuity, and . . . he left sources from which those who came after him could derive instructive principles." Hermogenes' Temple Artemis Leukophryene at Magnesia of about 150 B.C. revived the rigorous systems of grid column placement and proportion established by Pytheos in the Temple of Athena Polias at Priene, built about 335 B.C.. A dis-cussion of the rule oriented aspect of Hermogenes' architecture is found in "The didactic tradition":

Jerome J. Pollitt, *Art in the Hellenistic Age* (Cambridge: Cambridge University Press, 1986) pp. 242-247.

24. Vitruvius, *The Ten Books,* bk. II, introduction. The following translation of the Deinocrates story by Ingrid Rowland is taken from the ms. of a new illustrated and annotated edition of *The Ten Books,* which we are producing in collaboration.

In the days when Alexander was master of the world, Deinocrates, an architect full of clever ideas, set out from Macedonia for the royal encampment, eager to obtain Alexander's attention. From home he carried letters of recommendation from neighbors and friends, addressed to the king's generals, in order to facilitate his access to them. When these generals received him, he asked them politely to present him to Alexander as soon as possible. Though they promised to do so, they took their time about it, waiting for some suitable occasion. And so Deinocrates, thinking that the generals were simply toying with him, approached the garrison on his own. He was a tall man, handsome, with a fine face and immense dignity. Trusting, then, in those gifts of Nature, he went back to his room, undressed, and thoroughly oiled his body. Crowning his head with a poplar wreath, draping his left arm in a lionskin and brandishing a club in his right hand he strode before the tribunal where the king was hearing petitions. When the crowd began to take notice of this novelty, Alexander, too, looked Deinocrates' way. Impressed by the young man, the king ordered the crowd to make way for him to approach the tribunal, and asked who he was.

"Deinocrates," came the answer, "an architect of Macedon, who brings you ideas and plans worthy of your renown. I have a project, for example, to carve all Mount Athos into the image of a man. In his left hand I'll fashion the walls of a great city; in his right, a basin where the waters of all the rivers which run on that mountain will gather together and plunge into the sea."

Alexander, delighted with this idea, inquired immediately about the surrounding territory—were there farmlands to furnish this city with a steady supply of grain? When the king learned that food would have to be imported by sea, he said, "Deinocrates, I appreciate the ingenuity of this plan, but I also recognize that if someone were to found a colony there, his sanity would be called into question. A newborn baby cannot be nourished and grow without its nursemaid's milk; neither can a city grow without farmlands and the flow of their produce into town. Without resources, no city can maintain a dense population or safeguard its people. As much as I admire your design, I find its location deplorable—but I want to keep you with me, because I intend to make use of your talents.'' From then on Deinocrates never parted from the king, and followed him into Egypt.

Krautheimer, *The Rome of Alexander VII.* The drawing by Pietro da Cortona makes a delightful twist on the story of Dinocrates by depicting Pope Alexander VII as the ancient emperor and Cortona as the assistant to the now-clothed Hellenistic architect.

25. Vincent Scully, *The Earth, the Temple, and the Gods: Greek Sacred Architecture* (New Haven: Yale University Press, 1962), pp. 3-9. In contradiction to this statement, Scully interprets the differences of specific Doric peristyles as indicating a response to the character of various dedications.

26. John Onians, *Art and Thought in the Hellenistic Age: The Greek World View, 350-50 B.C.* (London: Thames and Hudson, 1979), pp. 72-79. Onians speculates on the origins of the concept of character in the orders during the Hellenistic period in ''Stylistic Choices in Architecture.''

27. Vitruvius, *The Ten Books,* bk. III, chap. I, 2-7: Analogy between the symmetry of a temple and a well-shaped man. Bk. III, chap. I, 4-8: Relation of the Corinthian to the physique and character of a maiden. Bk. I, chap. II, 5: Vitruvius's discussion of propriety is the context for relating the order of a building to the character of the god to whom it is dedicated.

Sebastiano Serlio, *The Five Books of Architecture, 1611,* bk. IV, facsimile (New York: Dover Publications, Inc., 1982).

28. Franco Borsi, *Bernini* (New York: Rizzoli, 1980) pp. 41-57.

29. Irving Lavin, *Bernini and the Unity of the Visual Arts* (Princton: Princeton University Press, 1981).

30. Connors, *Borromini and the Roman Oratory, Style and Society,* pp. 34-35.

31. Rudolph Wittkower, *Art and Architecture in Italy, 1600-1750* (New York: Penguin Books, 1978), pp. 205-206. See pp. 310-11 for Antonio Raggi's collaboration with other architects.

Borromini's approach to the use of programmatic sculpture is fully developed in his lantern and dome at Sant' Ivo alla Sapienza. John Beldon Scott interprets the combination of symbols as a statement of the concept of Divine Wisdom in:

''S. Ivo alla Sapienza and Borromini's Symbolic Language,'' *Journal of the Society of Architectural Historians* 41 (December 1982): pp. 299-317.

32. Erik Forssman, *Dorisch, Jonisch, Korinthisch; Studienüber den Gebrauch der Säulenordnungen in der Architektur des 16-18 Jahrhunderts* (Stockholm: Almquist & Wiksell, 1961, Wiesbaden: Friedr. Vieweg & Sohn, 1983). Forssman singles out the Tuscan order for the special significance it held in Flanders during the sixteenth and seventeenth centuries.

33. Maurice Culot, *La Laurentine e l'Invention de la Villa Romaine* (Paris: Editions du Moniteur, 1982).

Helen H. Tanzer, *The Villas of Pliny the Younger* (New York: Columbia University Press, 1924).

Architects have made reconstructions from the evocative ''Tuscan'' and ''Laurentian'' letters by Pliny since at least 1615. The Iñiguez and Ustarroz design for the Laurentian Villa is one of eleven projects completed for an exhibition sponsored by the *Institut Francais d'Architecture* in 1982, designed to test receptivity to the implications of a classical program. This design exudes little of the sensuous quality of place that Pliny's letter evokes, yet it is perhaps the most fundamentally classical scheme of all reconstructions submitted. Leon Krier's design for the same exhibition has been widely published. It is depicted in figure Intro-9. Culot's catalog surveys the historical reconstructions and updates Tanzer's excellent catalog.

34. Vitruvius, *On Architecture,* bk. IV, chap. I, 8-10, trans. Frank Granger (1932) (Cambridge: Harvard University Press, 1962) p. 209.

35. Theophile Homolle, ''L'Origine du Chapiteau Corinthian,'' *Revue Archèologique* (Paris, 1916), pp. 17-60.

Joseph Rykwert, "The Origin of the Corinthian Capital," *The Necessity of Artiface*, originally published in *Domus* 426 (May 1965): pp. 25-30.

These articles interpret the Vitruvian legend as an outgrowth of ancient burial customs.

36. Heinrich Bauer, *Korinthische Kapitelle des 4. und 3. Jahrhunderts v. Chr.* Professor Baurer has kindly allowed me to use his drawings for the Bassae, Tegea and Epidaurus capitals as a basis for my illustrations.

37. Andrew F. Stewart, *Skopas of Paros* (Park Ridge, N.J.: Noyes Press, 1977), p. 80.

38. William L. Macdonald, *The Architecture of the Roman Empire* (New Haven: Yale University Press, 1965), p. 98.

39. D. S. Robertson, *Greek and Roman Architecture,* (Cambridge: Cambridge University Press, 1969) pp. 161-62.

40. Antonio Giuliano, "Capitello Corinzio di Lesena (Senza n. inv.)," *Museo Nazionale Romano, Le Sculture 1,* 7 (Rome: De Luca Editore, 1984), pp. 399-400.

41. Guarino Guarini, *Architettura Civile,* pl. VIII.

Rudolf Wittkower, *Art and Architecture in Italy, 1600-1750,* pp. 406-10.

42. Robert Drews, *In Search of the Shroud of Turin: New Light on its History and Origins* (Totowa, N.J.: Rowman & Allanheld, 1984).

Ian Wilson, *The Shroud of Turin* (New York: Image Books, 1979).

43. Eugen von Mercklin, *Antike Figural Kapitelle* (Berlin: Walter de Gruyter & Co., 1962), pl. 385a.

44. Gisela M. A. Richter, *Catalog of Greek Sculptures in the Metropolitan Museum of Art* (Cambridge: Harvard University Press, 1954), p. 121. This enlarged Roman copy of a fourth-century B.C. Greek statue was discovered in Rome in 1631.

45. Robert Graves, "The First Labour: The Nemean Lion," *The Greek Myths, Vol. 2* (Harmondsworth: Penguin Books, 1983), pp. 103-107.

46. Francesco Azzurri, "Due Singolari Capitelli Scoperti presso la Riva del Tevere," *Bulletino della Commissione Archaeologica di Roma* (1892), pp. 175-78, pl. ix.

Antonio Giuliano, *Museo Nazionale Romano, Le Sculture,* I, 1 (Rome: De Luca Editore, 1984), pp. 264-65, 334-35.

Georg Lippold, *Die Skupturen des Vaticanischen Museums* (Berlin: Walter de Gruyter & Co., 1956), pp. 192-93, pl. 91.

D. Marchetti, "Di un antico molo per lo sbarco dei marmi riconosciuto sulla riva sinestra del Tevere," *Bulletino della Commissione Archaeologica di Roma* (1891), pp. 45-60.

I am grateful to John Beldon Scott for having arranged permission to move the Hercules Shrine architrave at the *Museo Nazionale Romano* for photographing and documenting it and the capitals. Darby Scott directed me to the publications after a visit to the *Museo* in 1970.

47. Robert Graves, "Omphale," *The Greek Myths, Vol. 2,* pp. 162-66. "It amused Omphale and Hercules to exchange clothes . . . Omphale put on his lion skin and he dressed in her purple gown. . . . Pan spread the rumor that the whimsical exchange of garments was habitual and perverse."

48. Axel Boethius, *Etruscan and Early Roman Architecture* (New York: Penguin Books, 1978), p. 139. Boethius calls this structure "a Hellenistic intruder upon the Roman scene" and speculates that "Roman Generals may have brought a Greek architect and the marble from Greece to Rome. . . ."

Donald Emrys Strong, "The Round Temple in the Forum Boarium," *Papers of the British School at Rome* (1960), pp. 9-31.

Friedrich Rakop and Heilmeyer Wolf-Dieter, *Der Rundtempel am Tiber in Rom.* (Mainz, W. Germany: P. von Zabern, 1973).

Lawrence Richardson discussed the recent attribution of this building to Hercules in a presentation at the American Academy in Rome in 1979.

49. Christian Norberg Schulz, *Late Baroque and Rococo Architecture* (New York: Harry N. Abrams, Inc., 1974), pp. 93-96.

50. Christian Norberg Schulz, *Kilian Ignaz Dientzenhofer e il Baroco Boemo* (Rome: Officina Edizione, 1968), pp. 108-9.

51. Paolo Portoghesi, *Barocco Latino Americano* (Rome: instituto Italo Latino Americano, 1980), p. 89.

52. George Kubler and Martin Soria, *Art and Architecture in Spain and Portugal and their American Dominions, 1500-1800* (Baltimore: Penguin Books, 1979).

53. Richard Krautheimer, *Early Christian and Byzantine Architecture* (Baltimore: Penguin Books, 1965), pp. 41-45, 111-13.

Karen Einaudi, *Ancient Roman Architecture* (Chicago: University of Chicago Press, Chicago Visual Library, 1980), fiche.

Hugh Plommer, *Ancient and Classical Architecture* (London: Longmans, Green and Co., 1956), pp. 356-65. This book has a fine review of the orders and ends with a sympathetic discussion of the transformation of classical architecture during the late Classical/Byzantine period.

CHAPTER 4

1. J. W. Goethe, *Italian Journey 1786-88*, trans. W. H. Auden, ed. Elizabeth Mayer (San Francisco: North Point Press, 1982), pp. 50-51. Joseph Connors kindly brought this passage to my attention.

2. Cesare Ripa, *Nova Iconologia* (Padova: P. P. Tozzi, 1618), "Academia" pp. 2-6, "Dottrina" p. 190, "Invenzione" pp. 330-331.

GLOSSARY

abacus pl. abaci: The general term for the uppermost element of a capital. The slab is square for Tuscan and Doric, rectangular with an ovolo or cyma reversa profile for Ionic, and a combination of astragal and cavetto shaped into four concave sides with diagonal horns for the Corinthian and Composite orders.

acanthus: A stylized carving of the *Acanthus mollis* leaf used as the most significant embellishment of the Corinthian capital.

aedicula pl. aediculae: The general term for a vertical composition of two columns supporting an entablature with a pediment or a pedimented portal or window; a shrine.

akroterion pl. akroteria: The pedestal blocks placed at the apex or lateral corners of a pediment upon which statuary or ornaments rest. Used less technically for the ornaments themselves, taking the triangular forms of a finial with a palmette, acanthus stalks, a disk (at the apex), or a sphinx or griffin at the corners.

alette: The portion of a pier visible on both sides of an engaged column or pilaster in the fornix motif.

ambulatory: An interior circular or U-shaped walkway around the sanctuary of a church.

annulets: The three stepped rings, or fillets, at the top of the neck in a Doric capital that form the transition to the echinus. Sometimes executed as grooves.

anta pl. ante: The representation of a pier articulated on the end of a spur wall to visually support the entablature, or on a wall paired with an adjacent column. The anta is similar in concept to a pilaster but was a Greek development for Doric and Ionic orders. The description of a temple type *in antis* refers to any number of columns forming a portico flanked by a pair of spur walls terminated with ante, e.g., dystyle in antis.

antefix: A decorated upright slab used to close or conceal the open end of a row of tiles which run across the lateral cornice of a gabled roof.

anthemion pl. anthemia: A repetitive floral motif of alternating palmette and lotus or honeysuckle forms linked by curved acanthus stalks used to embellish a cyma recta profile.

apophyge: A transitional curve that connects the cylinder of a column shaft to the fillet at the bottom of the shaft or to the astragal at the top. A similar transitional curve from a fascia to a fillet.

architrave: The beam that spans from column to column, epistyle.

archivolt: A molded casing around an arch with a distinct profile corresponding to the articulation of each order.

arris: The vertical ridge on a Doric column shaft formed by the intersection of two flutes.

ashlar: Squared building stone laid in a regular pattern to form a running bond.

astragal: A composite molding consisting of a roundel and a fillet that terminates the shaft zone of Tuscan, Ionic, Corinthian, and Composite columns. The molding is also found in other locations.

atlantes: Statues of men used to support a Doric entablature. Also called atlas or telamon.

attic base: a type of column base composed of a square plinth surmounted by a large torus, a scotia, and a smaller torus above. Originally developed to supplant the more delicate Ionic base types, it should be employed only with the Corinthian.

baldacchino: A permanent canopy supported by four columns.

balteus pl. baltei: A vertical molding that constricts the bolster of an Ionic capital.

baluster: The swelling support of a railing or balustrade.

base: The lowest element of a column, consisting of astragal, torus, scotia moldings, and a plinth.

bead and reel: Sculptural ornamentation of the roundel in Ionic, Corinthian, and Composite orders, consisting of oval beads alternating with a pair of disks set as though strung together.

Beaux Arts: The system of architectural education developed in the French Academy in Rome during the eighteenth century and formalized in Paris throughout the nineteenth century. Also a style of classical architecture taught and developed not only in France but throughout the United States from the 1890s through the 1930s. During the late 1920s it was the focus of debate between classical and modernist approaches to architecture.

bed mold: A general term for a molding that supports the soffit of a cornice.

bell: The flaring cylindrical core of Corinthian and Composite capitals.

bolster: The elastic sides of the Ionic volute. Also called pulvinus or pulvination.

boukranion: The sculpted skull of an ox used as a decorative element both in the Doric metope and continuous friezes.

bud: A sinuous tendril and bud on the bell of a Composite capital.

canalis: The gently concave area of the Ionic volute between two lines of the spiral and the cushion above the cymation.

canonical: Relating to rule; the currently "accepted" canon of proportion for a particular practice of classical architecture.

capital: The uppermost element of the column between shaft and entablature.

caryatid: Support, carved in the shape of a woman, for an Ionic entablature.

casing: A frame around an opening consisting of fasciae and moldings.

cathetus: The vertical axis of an Ionic volute from the radius of the eye to the beginning of the spiral, or an imaginary axial line through a column.

cathri: A pierced screen or metal railing formed by superimposing perpendicular and diagonal crosses.

cauliculus: The acanthus stalk from which the spiral and helix tendrils of the Corinthian capital emerge.

cavetto: A simple concave molding.

cella: The principal interior volume of a temple type building. Also called *naos.*

cincture: An astragal binding the shaft of a Solomonic column to separate various zones of ornamentation.

column: Cylindrical support consisting of base, shaft, and capital.

console: A vertical scroll bracket that supports both ends of a cornice above a door or window. A similar bracket developed from the keystone of an arch to support the architrave in the fornix motif.

corbel: a bracket that projects from a vertical surface to support a beam. A graduated succession of corbels form a corbelled arch or vault.

cornice: The uppermost component of the entablature that projects to represent the overhang of a roof.

corona: The vertical fascia of a cornice.

crepidoma: The stepped platform of a temple excluding the top step or stylobate.

cyma recta: An S-curve molding in which the concave section projects beyond the convex section and terminates with a perpendicular fillet.

cyma reversa: An S-curve molding in which the convex section projects beyond the concave section and has no perpendicular fillets.

cymation: A specialized term for the Ionic echinus. Also a diminutive for cyma, e.g., a small cyma reversa.

dentil: The closely spaced blocks that project to support the soffit of an Ionic cornice. They may represent a lattice system of interwoven small-scale beams in primitive construction.

die: The primary block of a pedestal left exposed between its base and cornice.

diminution: The decreased diameter of a column shaft at the neck or occasionally, less obviously, at the base.

Doric leaf: A tongue-shaped painted ornament for the hawksbeak molding.

double roundel: Two adjacent torus moldings.

dovetail tenon: A butterfly-shaped piece of wood inserted into two adjacent beams or panels to bind them together.

drip: An undercut in the soffit of a cornice that prevents water from being drawn across the soffit by surface tension.

echinus: The ovolo-shaped disk that forms the transition from cylindrical shaft to the rectilinear architrave in the Tuscan and Doric capitals. Its profile can range from quarter round to essentially conical.

egg and tongue: A repetitive carved motif for the ovolo molding. Eggs surrounded by a band alternate with a spearlike tongue. Egg and dart refers to examples that depict a pronged arrow.

entasis: The specific curvature of a column shaft created by decreasing the diameter from the full module to the neck with an accelerated rate of diminution.

epikranitis: The continuous profile at the top of a wall consisting of a broad fascia decorated with a meander capped by a hawksbeak ornamented with the Doric leaf pattern.

epistyle: The Greek term for architrave.

escutcheon: A decorative shield as a field for emblems. A cartouche.

eye: The convex disk at the vortex of an Ionic volute spiral.

extrados: The outermost molding of an archivolt.

fasces: A representation of Roman power consisting of an axe surrounded by a bundle of sticks bound with straps. Similar forms of sticks and bindings can ornament the torus of a Corinthian base.

fascia pl. fasciae: The vertical plane of an architrave.

femur pl. femora: The vertical surfaces of the triglyph left between the glyphs.

fillet: A narrow, flat surface used as a transition between convex and concave moldings, such as the fillet of an astragal or the fillet between the flutes of an Ionic or Corinthian column.

flank: The side of a building.

fleuron: The flower carved at the center of each face of the abacus in the Corinthian and Composite orders. It is oval in the Corinthian and rectangular in the Composite. The central element is the ovum of a flower surrounded by a fan of petals.

flute: The vertical, concave channels of a column shaft that narrow as the shaft diminishes. The various orders need not be fluted, and the Tuscan never is. Doric flutes are shallow and intersect in sharp arrises. The oval flutes of the Corinthian and Composite orders are separated by fillets.

fornix pl. fornices: A compositional system which superimposes the trabeated system of columns and entablature upon the arch and pier of arcuated construction.

frieze: The second register of the entablature. The Doric frieze is characterized by alternating triglyphs and metopes. In the Ionic, the frieze is optional, occasionally developed in a bulging form called *pulvinated.* The frieze is the area most receptive to decoration in all orders.

frieze cap: The fillet that runs above the Doric frieze is a simple bed mold.

geison block: The Greek term for the cornice member of an entablature.

glyph: The vertical channel of a triglyph cut in a variety of angles and terminations. A semiglyph is chamfered at the triglyph edges.

gutta pl. guttae: The six pegs inserted under the regula of the Doric architrave. They can be shaped as cylinders or truncated cones and pyramids. The nine pegs inserted into the underside of the mutule are also called guttae.

hawksbeak: a hook-shaped molding of the Doric order.

helix: The spiral tendrils symmetrical to the center line of the Corinthian capital. Also called *caulis.*

herm: 1. The combination of a human bust with a tapering pier roughly proportional to the body, occasionally including feet and male genitalia.

horn: The diagonally projecting "points" of the Corinthian and Composite orders. Although the horns ended in sharp angles in archaic capitals, they are usually chamfered due to the fragility of the sharp edges.

hypophyge: A scotia under an archaic Doric echinus cut to serve as a transition between the neck and echinus.

hypostyle: A space in which numerous columns are set out on a grid to support a roof, such as the "hall of many columns" in an Egyptian temple.

iconography: A system of literal meaning ascribed to figures and objects in which the visual cues represent stories and ideas and convey a narrative program. Human figures can take on allegorical meaning, such as the representation of Architecture. An object can be designated an emblem to symbolize an idea like as the association of the laurel with Apollo and representing achievement. The orders have a limited emblematic capacity through their traditional and perceptual associations with gender and character.

impost: The "capital" of a pier from which an arch springs.

interaxial span: The distance from axis to axis of columns, one module greater than the intercolumniation. The Ionic order may be planned interaxially due to its flexible entablature and tradition of grid planning. The Doric order does not relate to this system due to the link between column spacing and the position of triglyphs in the predetermined frieze.

intrados: The underside, or soffit, of an arch.

intercolumniation: The distance between columns measured from surface to surface of the full diameter of the shaft.

keystone: The uppermost component of an arch that completes the compressive system of the voussoirs. It can be emphasized by projection, texture, or treated as a console in the fornix motif to visually support the span of the architrave.

lotus: A fan-shaped decorative motif formed by symmetrically arranging lotus petals with a spreading curvature.

meander: The mazelike, or fretted, pattern of connected lines arranged in repetitive geometrical combinations.

metope: The square slab alternating with triglyphs in the Doric frieze. It is the only zone that accommodates figural or emblematic decoration in the Doric order.

modillion: An S-curved horizontal bracket that supports the soffit of the Corinthian cornice. It can be plain or richly ornamented with volutes, palmettes, and an acanthus cartouche.

monopteros: A templelike structure consisting only of columns and superstructure without a cella. Also monopteron.

mutule: The angled slabs visible underneath the doric soffit representing the tails of rafters. Mutules are centered over triglyphs and metopes and have eighteen guttae inserted in three regular lines. Mutules slope approximately 13° from the frieze cap. In the Tuscan order the *traiecturae mutulorum* is the secondary beam that rests on the architrave and projects to support the overhang of the gabled roof.

neck: The lowest register of the Tuscan and Doric capitals.

oculus: A circular hole in a dome that admits light.

ogival: Relating to pointed rather than full arch construction.

olive leaf cluster: The bunches of olive leaves sculpted to form the decoration of the Composite order.

opisthodomos: The rear chamber of a temple entered from the back side.

orthogonal: The perpendicular relationship between planes in a rectilinear building.

ovolo: A convex egg-shaped molding. When decorated, carved, or painted with egg and tongue.

palmette: A fan-shaped decorative motif formed by symmetrically arranging palm leaves with an upward curvature. Alternates with the lotus in the anthemion pattern, or employed diagonally to obscure the triangular cavity between the volute face and spiral in an Ionic capital.

paradigm: A model or standard for imitation; from the Greek *paradeigma.*

parapet: A low wall that extends above the roof of a building.

patera: A disk used to ornament a metope.

pedestal: A vertical block elaborated with a base and cornice, upon which a column stands. The proportions and profiles of moldings vary to correspond with the character of each order.

pediment: The triangular termination of a gabled roof formed by a horizontal corona and two raking cornices.

peristyle: The single colonnade that forms a portico all around the core of a temple type structure or around a court. Also called *pteron, peristasis.*

piazza: The Italian term for a public square. Piazzetta is a diminutive square.

pier: A vertical support, square or rectangular in plan.

pilaster: A two-dimensional representation of a column that stands out in slight relief from a wall. It is conceptually similar to an anta but developed with a squared version of the capital and base of its order.

pine cone: The oval drop that occupies the open corner of the dentil course in the Composite order.

plinth: The lowest element of a column base. The Ionic, Corinthian, and Composite orders have square slabs. The plinth of the Tuscan order is a cylindrical slab.

podium: The elevated platform upon which a building rests.

portico: A columned porch or walkway accessible from ground level.

profile: The contour of a molding.

propylon: A templelike gateway structure to a court or public open space.

prostyle: A type of temple in which columns form a portico only in front. Tetrastyle prostyle designates a portico with four columns.

pulvinate: Refering to the Ionic order in general. A pulvinated frieze swells with a convex surface, i.e., cushion-shaped.

purlin: The secondary timbers of a gable roof running longitudinally perpendicular and above the rafters.

quoins: Blocks of stone stacked in alternation at the corner of a building; may be imitated in other materials.

rafter: The principal timbers of a gable roof spanning from ridge pole to the walls and architrave.

raking cornice: The sloping cornice of a pediment. The corona and sima have the same profile as the lateral cornice when measured perpendicular to the slope.

regula: The horizontal block beneath each triglyph into which the guttae are inserted.

rustication: The intentional use of rough texture on masonry materials to convey a rudimentary or rustic character.

scamillus: A plain, low block upon which a column rests, neither as tall nor as articulated as a pedestal.

scotia: A concave molding formed by the radii of two quarter rounds—one twice the radius of the other.

semiglyph: The half glyphs at the edge of a triglyph.

serliana: A type of window or portico opening that consists of two rectangular openings separated by an arch. This term named for Sebastiano Serlio. Also called a Palladian arch.

serpentine flutes: The flutes that wind around a Solomonic column shaft.

shaft: The tapering cylindrical support of a column.

sima: The crowning molding or rain gutter of a cornice. The term does not specify a particular profile, which could be a cavetto, ovolo, or cyma recta.

sinking groove: The incised groove that separates the shaft from the capital in the Doric order. Also called *hypotrachelium.*

socle: A continuous wall base representing a podium upon which columns or pilasters stand.

spandrel: The roughly triangular surface between the archivolts of adjacent arches or between the archivolt and engaged column in the fornix motif.

spira: The lower disk of the Ionic base. The Samian profile is gently concave; the Ephesian is more complex.

split fillet: The joining of the fillets at the intersection of the raking and horizontal coronas in a pediment.

soffit: The underside of a cornice or architrave.

Solomonic column shaft: A serpentine column often elaborately embellished with relief decoration. During the Renaissance, ancient columns of this type were assumed to have come from the Temple of Solomon due to their richness.

string course: A horizontal band with various moldings used to define the stories of a building.

stylobate: The foundation for a range of columns exposed as the top step of a crepidoma.

superposition: The method of placing one order of columns above another.

taenia: The continuous fillet that caps the Doric architrave.

tholos pl. tholoi: A circular building with or without a peripteros.

toichobate: The continuous profiled base of a wall.

torus: The convex molding used in column bases.

trabeated: Describing a structure built with posts and lintels.

triglyph: The vertical member of the Doric frieze, consisting of a flat slab incised with vertical grooves.

tympanum: The triangular wall enclosed by a pediment.

via pl. viae: The narrow piece of soffit visible between the mutules of the Doric order.

volute: The spiral volume of the Ionic capital.

voussoir: The individual wedges of material that are built together to form an arch.